Northern Images

Northern Images

AUSTRALIA'S NORTHERN TERRITORY

PHOTOGRAPHY BY GUNTHER DEICHMANN   TEXT BY TIM COPE

Collins
Publishers
Australia

To my friends Gary and Marlene Wood

COLLINS PUBLISHERS AUSTRALIA
First published in 1989 by William Collins Pty Ltd
55 Clarence Street, Sydney, NSW 2000

Copyright © Gunther Deichmann, 1989

National Library of Australia
Cataloguing-in-Publication data:

Deichmann, G. (Gunther), 1951–
Northern images
ISBN 0 7322 0050 4
1. Northern Territory – Description and travel –
1976 – Views. I. Cope, Tim. II. Title.
994.2906'3'0222

Typeset in ITC Garamond Light by The Typographers, North Sydney
Produced by Mandarin Offset in Hong Kong

Contents

The Northern Territory

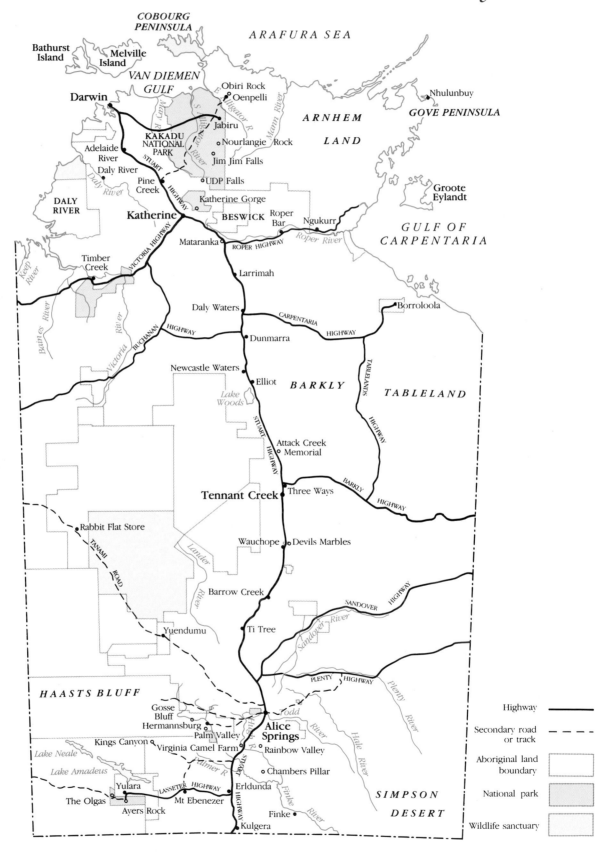

COBOURG
PENINSULA

ARAFURA SEA

Bathurst
Island

Melville
Island

*VAN DIEMEN
GULF*

Obiri Rock
Oenpelli

Nhulunbuy

Darwin

ARNHEM

GOVE PENINSULA

Jabiru

LAND

KAKADU
NATIONAL
PARK

Nourlangie Rock

Adelaide
River

Jim Jim Falls

Daly River

UDP Falls

Pine
Creek

Groote
Eylandt

Katherine Gorge

*DALY
RIVER*

Katherine

BESWICK

Roper
Bar

Ngukurr

*GULF OF
CARPENTARIA*

Mataranka

ROPER HIGHWAY

Roper River

Timber
Creek

Larrimah

Daly Waters

CARPENTARIA

Borroloola

HIGHWAY

Dunmarra

Newcastle Waters

BARKLY

TABLELAND

Elliot

*Lake
Woods*

Attack Creek
Memorial

Tennant Creek

Three Ways

Rabbit Flat Store

Wauchope

Devils Marbles

Barrow Creek

SANDOVER

HIGHWAY

Yuendumu

Ti Tree

Sandover River

PLENTY HIGHWAY

Plenty River

HAASTS BLUFF

Gosse
Bluff

Hermannsburg

Palm Valley

Alice
Springs

Kings Canyon

Virginia Camel Farm

Rainbow Valley

Lake Neale

Lake Amadeus

Chambers Pillar

Yulara

LASSETER HIGHWAY

Erldunda

SIMPSON

The Olgas

Mt Ebenezer

DESERT

Ayers Rock

Finke

Kulgera

Highway	————
Secondary road or track	– – – –
Aboriginal land boundary	
National park	
Wildlife sanctuary	

Introduction

The Northern Territory is a recent creation. A couple of hundred years ago it simply didn't exist. In its place lay a vast amorphous land, unscathed by politics and devoid of any boundary except the sea. The first humans to endure here created a culture that survived for longer than any other in the world. By the time the first urban communities of Western civilisation began to appear at the eastern end of the Mediterranean, the Australian Aborigines had already been living in a well-balanced communal society for thousands of years. They were the Territory's first explorers and its first pioneers. Their relationship with the land began at least 40 000 years ago at which time the world was in the grip of its great Ice Age. Several times during this period massive ice-sheets up to 3000 metres thick advanced from the polar regions, consuming land and sea. The level of the oceans dropped by as much as 150 metres. The early Aboriginal adventurers set out from Asia and used rafts to cross the short reaches of shallow water between the islands of the archipelago to the south. Beyond them lay the huge combined land-mass of Australia and New Guinea. Once they reached the last island in the chain all that remained was a voyage of a hundred kilometres. Inevitably the last passage was crossed and a great continent discovered.

And so the Aborigines became the first people to face the challenge of survival in the Northern Territory, and the first to meet it. Much later, in the 17th century, Dutch navigators touched upon the northern coast during their domination of the South Seas. But they did not stay, or even claim the land for their sovereigns since there was no profit to be gained from it. Who knows who else may have visited the Aborigines during the intervening ages? Perhaps a Chinese naval captain or an Arab trader blown off course! Fishermen from Macassar in the Celebes certainly visited the Arnhem Land coast for at least two centuries until a white administration banned them in 1906. The Aborigines still sing Macassan songs and there is abundant evidence of the interaction between the two peoples. The sailors arrived each year with the monsoon winds and got the Aborigines to help them collect and cure trepang, a sea slug prized as a gastronomic delicacy in China. They camped ashore for the summer, then returned with their valuable cargo to the flourishing markets of the East Indies.

The Macassans came and went in considerable numbers but their impact on Aboriginal culture was gentle and isolated. Not so British colonialism, which struck the same culture a blow which threw it off balance and changed it forever. Initially, the extremes of the Northern Territory were more than a match for the greatest empire of the century. In 1824 the Colonial Office reached out to establish a hold on northern Australia; five long, nightmarish years later it let go again. On two other occasions it attempted to establish trading posts on the coast but these also ended in failure. The Northern Territory acquired its shape only as sturdier British colonies were founded around it.

These colonies took what they wanted and left an area of stunning topographical diversity, uninhabited by a single European. South Australia made an attempt to settle the Territory in 1864 but its garrison at the mouth of the Adelaide River disintegrated within two years. Another two years later a much more efficient expedition left Adelaide to survey a settlement at Port Darwin, first discovered 30 years before. Unseen land parcels which had been sold in London were pegged. By the skin of its teeth and the grace of God this fifth settlement survived. Administrators and policemen were sent north and a telegraph line built from one end of the continent to the other. Things soon picked up momentum when gold was discovered. Cattle were driven overland from Queensland. The lonely outpost at Port Darwin, almost inaccessible by any route but sea, became a capital like no other. It was a place of wild and turbulent character. Today it is a vibrant city which has found its identity in the South-East Asian economic region. Its early survival was primarily responsible for the second great wave of pioneering settlement in the Territory.

But the entire history of human inhabitation of the Northern Territory is infinitesimal compared to the history of the place itself. Not only is the Territory's basic structure so ancient that it defies comprehension but its features are among the oldest in the world. They include the astonishing landforms known today as Ayers Rock, the Olgas, the Katherine Gorges and the Arnhem Land plateau. These landforms lay unnamed through the ages until humans came and ascribed to each

a reason for being. Some explanations are recent and geological in nature but others evolved in the religion of the first Australians, long before the invention of science. The Aborigines' mythology emphasised the deep bond between themselves and the land, including all its features. It was a bond forged in the Dreamtime, when the world began. Humans, animals, plants and the physical formations of the land were all caught up in the story of genesis. A father explained it to his son as a gift of self-identity. Many explanations of creation among the various tribes of the Territory revolved about an awesome, rainbow-coloured snake. The northern people had one such story.

In the Dreamtime the land was flat and barren. There were people but there were no animals, birds, trees, plants, rivers or hills. The gigantic rainbow snake awoke and set out to look for his own tribe. He travelled north across the dim, featureless landscape and as he went he created mountains, rivers and gorges with his mighty slithering. He found his tribe in the north and taught them new rituals. But then he committed an atrocity and fled to the only natural mountain in the land. The people followed and the tree goanna brothers climbed up to where the snake lay sleeping on the summit. They cut his belly open to release two boys whom he had swallowed and these immediately turned into rainbow lorikeets. The rainbow snake awoke and in his wounded fury he threshed the mountain to pieces, creating thunder and lightning and killing many members of his tribe with falling boulders. The boulders became hills and the men and women who were most frightened of all transformed themselves into the animals, birds, insects and plants we know today. The great snake then slithered into the sea, where he remains. That is how the land got its basic characteristics.

When the first scientists came to the Northern Territory in the 19th century they measured and studied things and made trained conclusions. The geologists' report is one of violent volcanic eruptions, of buckling movements in the earth's crust and of prehistoric inland seas which left hardening sediments in their wakes. It's a report in which changes are identified by eras, periods, epochs and ages and the basic unit of measurement is a million years. The Northern Territory is on the eastern edge of one of the world's most ancient geological shield zones. It is an extremely old part of the earth's crust and has a hard, crystalline, Pre-Cambrian base rock. The oldest rocks are near Western Australia and have existed for two and a half billion years. On a scale of world history, those rocks appeared at a point exactly halfway between the formation of the earth and the present, give or take a hundred million years. The Territory is literally half as old as time. Eastern Australia came later.

The massive plateau of Arnhem Land, in the north-east of the Territory, started to form more than 2000 million years ago. Sea-levels and coastlines fluctuated and were different from those we know today. The plateau took shape as water deposited sand and mud in layers over the ages. When the seas receded and the earth turned on the heat and the pressure, this sedimentary material became sandstone, conglomerate and quartzite. It was pushed up by earthquakes and worn down by rain. Molten rock seethed up from the guts of the earth and added a new dimension to the landscape, bringing valuable minerals to the surface through weak lines in its crust. Two rivers of rich igneous rock traverse the Territory and were thrown up in this way. One starts at Mount Isa in Queensland and arcs up through Arnhem Land into the Kimberley Ranges of Western Australia. The other curls south from the Kimberleys back through central Australia toward Queensland. They are rivers of gold, tin, tantalite, silver, lead, zinc, copper, manganese, wolfram, iron and uranium. Unnoticed and unsought by the Aborigines, these metals lay undisturbed until a little more than a hundred years ago. The giant Ranger mine now extracts uranium in the shadow of the magnificent sandstone escarpment that is the western edge of the Arnhem Land plateau.

At the other end of the Territory a similar tale unfolds of sedimentary and igneous forces. In fact the symbol of the Centre, Ayers Rock, is a product of both. The oldest rocks in the region began to form more than 1700 million years ago – granites, schists, and so on. Much later they were folded into mountain ranges by enormous earthquakes. The striking MacDonnell Ranges which stretch out to the west from Alice Springs were formed in this way. About 600 million years ago central Australia was covered by a vast, shallow inland sea. It washed over low outcrops and lapped against the sides of ancient mountains. As it did so it laid layer upon layer of rock fragments and sand on its bed. These sediments were compressed into stratified sandstone and became a type of rock cemented by brown and red oxides of iron and containing pieces of quartz and felspar. It was from this sedimentary strata that Ayers Rock and the Olgas were made.

Those two remarkable landforms were created about 450 million years ago when certain parts of the sandstone plain of central Australia blew up, shattered by immense subterranean forces. The earth's crust buckled and broke into pieces. Some bits were pushed up on end so that the sediments of ages pointed to the sky. Ayers Rock was one of these. The great ridges you can walk upon today are its eroded layers. Ayers Rock emerged at an angle of about 85 degrees, the Olgas at about 20 degrees. They were originally much bigger but centuries without number have worn them into their present bosomy shapes and created a plain of red sand all around. Theoretically these landmarks will disappear altogether one day although, in their presence, such a thing is impossible to imagine. Ayers Rock is literally rusting away. Small pieces flake off it constantly in a chemical weathering process. It is the world's greatest monolith and the only phenomenon of its kind. This is because, unlike the Olgas and other formations, it has none of the planes of weakness which cause big rocks to split into smaller rocks. And in fact there is probably twice as much of Ayers Rock under the ground as there is above it. It is little wonder that it totally dominated the lives of the Pitjantjatjara Aborigines. For them, every scar, every cave, every waterhole at its base was a sacred place full of meaning, a story with its origins in the Dreamtime.

Other ancient seas covered the Territory as well. The Barkly Tableland is a flat region near the Queensland border overlaid by the hardened sediments of a once-encroaching ocean. But here the results are limestone, made from the skeletons of minute plants and animals laid down in the warm shallow seas of the Cretaceous Period. Beneath the now-dry Tableland lies underground water in an artesian basin. Water comes close to the surface in places throughout the interior and fills the wells which kept countless generations of desert people alive.

Many of the geological events that moulded the Territory happened billions of years ago when the only living things on earth were bacteria and algae. Consequently, the rocks created during those early epochs contain no fossils. The 1800-million-year-old rocks of the Katherine Gorges fall into the pre-fossil category. Yet the world had all its modern mammals before the walls of the gorges started to form 25 million years ago. Initially a seasonal stream found a channel through the grid-like fissures of the Arnhem Land plateau. Each subsequent year the fissures became fractionally deeper. The stream gradually evolved into something much bigger as other waters were drawn into it. Now, every wet season, the Katherine River roars through the gorges beneath 60 metres or more of its own handiwork.

The Northern Territory has a fairly even geological structure, but the plant life of the area is anything but uniform. In the north are great swamps teeming with succulent plants; in the south, the sparse, wiry and tenacious species which have managed to resist extinction in the ferocious heat of the central Australian deserts. Climate is the key. Although almost all of the Territory lies above the Tropic of Capricorn in one of the world's torrid zones, the climates on the coast and in the interior are as different as a water lily and a clump of spinifex. When the Australian summer arrives at the end of November, the rain comes to the tropical Top End of the Northern Territory. It batters the landscape every day for three or four months of the year. Thunderstorms come most often in the afternoon, enact their violent ritual, and subside. The city of Darwin and nearby Melville Island experience more thunderstorm activity than anywhere else in Australia – more than 80 days of it each year. The Top End is also prone to the terrifying energy of periodic tropical cyclones. The wet season dumps more than 1500 millimetres of rain on the far north in a normal season. In the record-breaking 1974–75 summer the rainfall exceeded 2200 millimetres: more than 85 inches. On the Arnhem Land plateau, in Kakadu National Park and upon the savannah plains south of Darwin, this water revitalises a landscape starting to crack up after a long dry season. It is also a great erosive force, shooting over waterfalls in the escarpment country and bursting rivers on the floodplains below. Everything turns green in an instant. The animals and birds rejoice.

Further down the Territory, in the Victoria River region near Western Australia and the tableland near Queensland, the rain comes at the same time of year but there is less of it. These areas are characterised by grassy plains and light woodlands but further south the rain diminishes and the semi-desert of spinifex and mulga takes over. Central Australia's rainfall is the complete antithesis of the northern wet season. It is usually low, invariably isolated and always utterly unpredictable. It's said that water has flowed along the whole sandy length of the Finke River only twice this century. In the northern part of the Centre, wayward thunderstorms will bring some summer rain; south of Alice Springs the averages plummet to a hundred millimetres or less. In some years it simply doesn't rain at all. In other years the annual allowance might come in a single day. Summer temperatures soar far beyond those of the north. In the Top End the average maximum hovers close to 30 degrees Celsius all year round while humidity crawls from one extreme of the scale to the other. In the interior, summer days of 40 degrees and winter nights of below zero are not uncommon. Given a climate such as this and a sandy terrain, it's a wonder anything grows in the desert at all!

But the Centre is well endowed with plants that have adapted perfectly to arid conditions. All have techniques for conserving precious moisture. Some rotate their leaves by day to avoid the full glare of the sun, others simply have spikes or needles instead of leaves. Almost 400 of the Territory's 2700 indigenous plant species manage the desert remarkably well: the mulga and bloodwood, the witchetty and emu bush, the ghost gums and acacia on the dry creek banks and the spinifex grass which holds the low red sand dunes in place. When it does rain, the desert becomes a place of incomparable beauty, covered in the most ephemeral of pink and blue wildflowers and soft, sudden grasses. Their seeds lie dormant in the sand for months or years, waiting for the right amount of water. In Palm Valley and Kings Canyon, plants which grew millions of years ago during a wetter era have survived because of the steady seepage of water through porous layers of sloping sandstone. In Palm Valley stand the unique *Livistona mariae* palm and the MacDonnell Range Cycad. Another seventeen living fossils grow in Kings Canyon.

The deserts of the Centre are nothing like the vast, sandy wastes of popular legend. Not only are they covered in plants but they provide a habitat for a surprising number of animals. Little creatures are constantly moving among the spinifex: the ant-eating echidna, the bizarre thorny devil, hopping mice, the snakes

which eat them and countless species of insects. Birds of prey hover above. Other birds rest in the shade provided by low scrubby trees and the ghostly white-barked gums: wrens, finches, honeyeaters, budgerigars, cockatoos, galahs and parrots. Big red kangaroos graze on the grasslands, emus wander among the dunes and wallabies and dingoes take refuge on rocky outcrops. There are even frogs in the desert. One species can remain buried a metre below the surface of a dried-up pool for up to three years, waiting for rain. When the pool fills up the frog emerges from its tomb to breed. The tadpoles have just enough time to mature before the water evaporates and the cycle once more is completed. Among all these native species roam the wild camels, horses, goats, donkeys, rabbits and foxes which are the progeny of animals brought to Australia by Europeans. Cattle graze in the better-grassed regions. Some of these animals are found throughout the Territory but, generally speaking, the north has an entirely different flora and fauna.

The geographic characteristics of the Top End are coastal mangrove forest, monsoon forest, savannah woodland, grassland and swamps, many of which have more in common with Indonesia than other parts of the Territory. There are a few big trees and only small patches of rainforest where there is permanent water. Beside rivers and on the floodplains are pandanus palms and paperbark trees. Grasses grow to be more than 3 metres high during the wet season. In Kakadu National Park, located at the centre of the Top End, a great many aspects of the geography and wildlife of the region are collected. It has the rugged escarpment country of the plateau stretching east into Arnhem Land, the undulating woodlands to the west of the escarpment and the vast, flooded plains of the East and South Alligator River regions. When the rains come in November or December, the torrents swell permanent billabongs and fill up the dry ones. Watergrasses and lilies spring to life from dormant seeds, and ephemeral flowers spread over the waters in a delicate covering of yellow.

A thousand species of plants have been recorded in Kakadu and there are also 10 000 species of insects, 22 species of frogs, 43 species of fish, 50 species of mammals and at least 270 species of birds (a third of all Australian species). Some of the birds, such as the lavender-flanked wren and the yellow chat, are rare and found only in the Park. Others – the jabiru, magpie goose and burdekin duck – are less specialised, although confined to tropical parts of Australia. About 80 species breed in the Northern Hemisphere and visit Kakadu for the wet season when it is winter at home. Kakadu has every imaginable type of brilliantly coloured dragonfly, butterfly, beetle, cricket and grub. It also has the mosquitoes, sandflies and termites which so bedevilled the first European settlers. Near the escarpment live rock wallabies and agile wallabies, reptiles and snakes. Saltwater crocodiles live in all types of waters. They are ideally suited to the rivers, estuaries and coastal billabongs of the entire Top End. These ancient creatures evolved with the dinosaurs more than 220 million years ago. They took to the water in the Triassic Period and survived whatever it was that extinguished the dinosaurs about 70 million years ago. They are frightful creatures – aggressive, armoured reptiles that grow to lengths of 7 metres or more. There are also smaller, freshwater crocodiles which eat fish rather than land-based mammals or humans.

There are some animals exclusive to the north which are feral descendants of beasts brought to Australia for agricultural or haulage purposes by European settlers. Among them are wild buffaloes and pigs which have done untold damage to some of the region's most delicate wetland ecology. Sixteen buffaloes were brought to the Cobourg Peninsula from Timor in 1827 to serve the needs of the second British settlement on the northern coast. When the settlement was abandoned two years later the animals ran wild. The same story was repeated in subsequent settlements. If the British loathed the humidity and the swampy landscape, the buffaloes loved it. It was just like home. They multiplied without restraint until their numbers reached 300 000 and they covered every area of lowland country in the far north. They have now been removed from Kakadu and its ecology saved. A campaign is under way to eradicate them altogether.

Into the organic frenzy of the Kakadu landscape came the first Australian Aborigines. They walked across the land bridge from New Guinea or paddled across the sea from Timor and other islands. They found plenty to eat in the lagoons and woodlands of the north, although food may have been as plentiful in the lands from which they came. Gradually they fanned out across the whole continent. Only after tens of thousands of years did their occupation of Australia start to resemble the pattern which existed when the white settlement started. Large populations lived in the places where their forefathers had arrived, like in the Top End of the Territory. They hunted for succulent barramundi in the rivers, for turtles and dugongs in the sea and for wallabies and reptiles on the land. Because they did not have to look far for sustenance they were able to stay in one place and build waterproof, paperbark shelters to protect themselves from monsoons. Tribal estates in the tropical north were often only of a few hundred square kilometres, owing to the abundance of food and the high population density. Conversely, in the central and western deserts, where food and water were scarce, tribal estates extended over many thousands of square kilometres. Wherever people lived in the desert they were frugal, nomadic bands, dominated by the needs of survival.

One thing all tribes had in common was a deep and complex attachment to the land. God sat not in heaven but upon the earth. The land bore its people and nurtured them but it could also be savage and unkind. It demanded respect, as parent from a child, but gave love in the form of life. All its parts, even the wind which blew over it and the water which lay under it, were aspects of the eternal union of land and people. All this was explained in mythology and reinforced in ritual. At the beginning and end of each human life lay the bosom of the earth. If proper burial rites were carried out, immortality was guaranteed in the spiritual realm of the Dreaming among the familiar features of one's estate. Every human spirit belonged to a particular place where an ancestral creation had occurred during the Dreamtime. Many marks on the land had this special significance. Some were awesome like Ayers Rock and the Ruined City of Arnhem Land, others were simply a depression in the ground. Today they are referred to as sacred sites.

Tribes were made up of several loosely related groups, or bands, each a basic social unit made up of a few families. There were an estimated six hundred tribes in Australia in prehistoric times, 126 of them in the Northern Territory. There were about two hundred separate languages and countless different dialects. The Aborigines had a complex system of kinship which blurred the distinctions between brothers and cousins, mothers and aunts, grandfathers and great uncles, and so on. They had no appointed leaders. The older men made decisions and were the custodians of secret and religious folklore. Next in seniority were the older women, not young men. Children were given a lot of affection and free-dom. They played traditional games and imitated their parents. Boys had toy spears and girls miniature digging sticks. Each day they learned a little more of bushcraft and eventually they became expert trackers. Art, music and dancing were integral parts of their lives and even as children they took their places in ritual ceremonies. They learned about their own traditions, although a young man could not know everything his grandfather knew until he was the same age. Before him lay a long cultural education. When he was aged between 12 and 14 years he was brought into the adult male world of ritual and responsibility by initiation. This important event was confirmed in a secret ceremony and symbolised by incisions cut on his body. After this he began to learn more deeply about tribal laws and ceremonial rituals, which he was expected to memorise and guard for following generations. Many of these rituals were concerned with fertility and the continuing supply of foods on the land. He carried hundreds of songs and dances in his head. His culture demanded that he conform to these arrangements, and the punishments dealt out for religious and kinship transgressions could be severe. He was supremely superstitious. Disasters were attributable to the sorcery of evil spirits or improperly observed rituals. Magic was used to fight off supernatural threats and to cure sickness. Part of this magic was the practice of pointing the bone, a symbolic death curse.

The desert women harvested seeds, tubers, berries and fruits and provided a reliable and varied diet upon which their families could subsist during lean times. They hunted out witchetty grubs and honey ants, collected water and used natural fibres to weave bags, baskets and ornaments. They used specialised tools such as grinding stones, digging sticks and winnowing dishes while their husbands carried spears, spearthrowers and boomerangs to stalk kangaroos and smaller game. The men also hunted emus, goannas and snakes. They knew the best woods for making various tools, ceremonial artefacts and musical instruments, and where to find flints for the cutting edges of chisels and knives. They made fire by rubbing a hard wood against a soft wood. When they had speared an animal they cooked it in an underground oven by lighting a fire in a pit and covering the carcass with hot stones and earth. They knew when it was time to suspend hunting and gathering near a waterhole in order to conserve animal life. All this knowledge was part of an inherited wisdom which had belonged to them from time immemorial.

In the north of the Territory, people were similarly attuned to their landscape but the climate was kinder to living things. White people often recognise only two seasons in the tropics: wet and dry. But the Arnhem Land Aborigines identified six, each heralded by natural events, like the gusty inland winds which flatten tall grasses after the rains have gone and the fruiting of native plums. The people wore no clothes to speak of. Men hunted fish with traps and nets as well as with spears. In some cases fish were killed by poisoning small pools with toxic leaves. Coastal tribes found their food in the sea more readily than on the land. They ate fish, shellfish, crabs, turtles, dugongs, and even small crocodiles. They made bark canoes. After the Macassans showed them the technique of hollowing out a log to make a dugout canoe they made those too. The women collected vegetable foods and small animals from swamps and used the leaves of pandanus palms to weave baskets, bags and mats. There was more food in the north and consequently more time for music, craftsmanship and art. The men of Arnhem Land made highly decorated musical instruments and painted on bark and rock surfaces. They recorded the most prominent things in their lives: the animals they hunted, the gods they feared, and themselves.

More than a thousand Aboriginal art sites can be seen today along the base of the Arnhem Land escarpment. The most ancient surviving paintings are at least 24 000 years old. New ones are still being created. At Obiri and Nourlangie Rocks in Kakadu National Park there are galleries containing hundreds of refined and skilful paintings. Many are still quite brilliant. Their colours are white and red clays, yellow ochres and black charcoal. Their styles and subjects vary according to their period. Some are primitive figures or stencils of hands, others are painted in the X-ray or the mimi style. This art reflects changing food sources, as the Kakadu landscape acquired its floodplains between 10 thousand and one thousand years ago. Other reflections are more modern: the praus of the Macassans and the frigates and guns of the Europeans. Dominating them all are depictions of the great spirits of the Dreaming: gods in the form of totems.

In its tangible form a totem was a particular animal, plant or element. It symbolised the spirit of creators and ancestors, some of whom had existed as people in the dawn of time but had been transformed, like the tree goanna brothers, into features of the landscape. A totem acted as an agent of communication between a tribe and its deities. It was also an emblem. It bestowed a tribal identity and told of tribal origins. Before religious ceremonies, men, women and children painted their faces and bodies and put on headdresses and anklets of feathers and leaves to identify with their totems. As they made the ritual movements of their dances they mimicked animals and acted out the spiritual relationships enshrined in mythology.

These symbolic performances occurred throughout the Territory. In the desert regions they related especially to the continuing supply of vegetable food, animals and water. Other important themes were marriage, fertility and the afterlife. In the Centre, totems were the only pictorial component of art, since the pre-occupation of tribes with survival was all-consuming. The astringency of the surviving rock art is a stark contrast to the lively Kakadu cave paintings. Desert artists took their subjects from mythology and left no mirror of their everyday lives. Sacred line designs were made in the sand, painted on bark and carved in wood. Unless they were engraved on stone or painted in one of the region's infrequent caves, they did not endure. The art of the Centre reflects a culture totally insulated in the heart of an intractable continent. In Arnhem Land, the Macassans gave the northerners tamarind trees, tobacco, iron tools, dugout canoes and venereal disease. But they also gave them a certain worldliness and a partial immunity to cultural shock. The arrival of European settlers was never as cataclysmic for the Top Enders as it was for the delicately poised lives of the inland people.

Aboriginal people needed the barest collection of possessions. They did not theorise about the meaning of existence. They had a human and an earth mother to care for them and a place in the world, made substantial by their tradition. They did not perceive a hierarchy in nature, nor consider themselves superior to animals. It never occurred to them to appoint regional leaders or organise armies to guard against marauding empires. They might not have had a sense of national unity or inter-tribal loyalty but they did have an island to themselves. It was a world all of its own. While an endless succession of cultures and empires lived and died like mayflies on the other side of the real world, Aboriginal society carried on as it had done for millennia. Always it adapted to gradually changing conditions; that is, until a change too vast and too sudden occurred. The change came with the arrival of the British, who had probed the South Pacific and claimed Australia during a bristling competition for colonial lands with their time-honoured adversary, the French.

The Dutch were the first Europeans to record Australia's northern shores. Willem van Colster sailed onto the Northern Territory coast by accident aboard the *Arnhem* in 1623. The Dutch had established themselves as the masters of trade in the East Indies in 1602 and Willem Jansz had seen the east coast of Australia in 1606. Ironically, Sir Francis Drake sailed through a passage north of New Guinea in 1580, unaware that the world's largest island lay to the south. Portuguese and Spanish ships preceded the famous Elizabethan Englishman and also missed Australia. Abel Tasman sailed Australia's entire northern coast from Cape York to the north-west corner of Western Australia in 1644. He reported back to his masters that there was nothing profitable to be taken from it and the Dutch lost interest. It was not until 1802 that Matthew Flinders came to chart the same shores for the British. He named the northern region Arnhem Land after the first European ship to find it.

The first Australian colony of New South Wales had been established in 1788 and its western boundary included a third of the modern Northern Territory. The rest of Australia was recognised as New Holland, a Dutch discovery of uncertain sovereignty. A remarkable young navigator named Phillip Parker King surveyed the coast of the Northern Territory from 1818 and recommended Port Essington as a good harbour and a fine place for a trading post. The British were already alarmed that French navigators had followed in Flinders' wake and they were determined to carry the naval superiority they had won at Trafalgar as far as possible. The British were the dominant sea power of the 19th century and the new masters of the East Indies, supplanting the Dutch who had themselves supplanted the Spanish and Portuguese sea powers of the 16th century. Napoleon had been dead just three years when the first of three British attempts at northern settlement was made at Fort Dundas on Melville Island in 1824. It stood just a hundred-odd kilometres north of where Darwin is today. The boundaries of New South Wales were redefined to incorporate it and any thoughts of Dutch ownership were cast aside. The outpost sat there, waiting to become a great trading post like Singapore, but it never happened. For the five years before it was abandoned, its soldiers, wives and convicts lived lives of unfulfilled hope and unremitting misery. Some were killed by Tiwi islanders, whose hostility to white men had its origins in the brutal raids of Portuguese slave traders. Savage retribution was dealt out by the garrison in some instances. The fear of native attack added to the afflictions of humidity, fever and biting insects, and combined with the terrible isolation of a place visited infrequently by supply ships, made the island seem like some far-flung corner of hell. Many of the garrison's inhabitants fell prey to tropical diseases and died. Others became deranged. Termites devoured anything made of wood and endless petty quarrels undermined morale.

Britain established another outpost in 1827 when it became apparent that Fort Dundas was not achieving the desired results. The second settlement, located at Raffles Bay on the Cobourg Peninsula, fared a little better. Relations with the Aborigines of the mainland became cordial and it appeared that some trade might eventuate when the Macassans arrived as usual for the wet season. Nevertheless, Britain decided to abandon both settlements in 1829. No further attempt was made for years. But thoughts of trade and the determination to prevent the French from establishing themselves in the region led to the establishment of another settlement in 1838. This one was at Port Essington, a beautiful but shallow natural harbour on the Cobourg Peninsula. The following year the *Beagle* paid a visit and sailed on to discover the north's only deep water harbour at Port Darwin, named after the great naturalist who had once sailed aboard the ship. Port Essington's planners dreamed of wide streets, great public buildings and a prosperous city but the settlers were beset by problems from the start. They found the soil of the region poor and almost useless for the agriculture they were used to, although tropical fruits flourished. Fresh water was scarce and periodic cyclones unleashed havoc.

The settlers began to feel many of the same soul-destroying miseries which had helped to defeat Fort Dundas. Some died of malaria and cholera brought from the East Indies. Those who remained did enjoy a friendly relationship with the Iwaidja Aborigines of the peninsula and for them that was a blessing. But in a story repeated time after time throughout the Pacific Islands and Australia, the Aborigines died in vast numbers from introduced diseases, including common influenza. They had not the slightest immunity. The garrison's commandant wrote to England that in one short period sixty or seventy local Aborigines had died. It was this kind of attrition among native tribes which led the British Government to conclude that the Aborigines were a dying race and would eventually disappear.

For its residents, Port Essington was a place of torment and failed dreams but in the eyes of one visitor it was a paradise. That may well have been because he almost died of starvation along the way. He was Ludwig Leichhardt, a Prussian naturalist and one of the first two European explorers to enter the Northern Territory by land. The other was Charles Sturt, who ventured into the Simpson Desert in search of an inland sea. Leichhardt left Brisbane in 1844 and travelled west, eventually marvelling at the wonders of Kakadu before passing on and reaching Port Essington in December 1845. He disappeared during an expedition three years later and was never heard of again. The Port Essington settlement itself ceased to exist in 1849. Its consistently low morale and lack of economic progress had convinced the Colonial Office to abandon it. In a bitter farewell, the settlers demolished their garrison and boarded the ship which had come to take them home. That marked the end of Britain's endeavours to settle the northern coast. It had proclaimed the colony of North Australia only three years before and it would be a quarter of a century before the inclination for northern settlement stirred again.

South Australia had been created as an independent British colony in 1834 and its territory carved out of New South Wales. Its ready-made western boundary was the border of Western Australia and its northern limit a line ruled east–west arbitrarily across the middle of the continent. These strokes on the map gave the Northern Territory its western and southern definitions, although at that time it was still a nameless part of New South Wales. When Queensland separated itself from the mother colony in 1859 and finally decided its borders in 1862, the Northern Territory was separated from its neglectful parent altogether. It acquired an eastern boundary and a definite physical shape, five times greater in size than Britain. It covered more than one and a quarter million square kilometres and was an undeveloped tract of continent which none of Australia's founding colonies had particularly wanted. Only the British had attempted to do anything with it. In political terms it was not so much a place as a vacuum.

But South Australia had already begun to take an interest in the outline of emptiness beyond its northern frontier. Within a few years of its establishment, Adelaide had become a vigorous, prosperous city. One of its wealthy self-made businessmen was James Chambers, who was convinced that a new fortune was to be made by discovering pastoral lands to the north. In 1855 Augustus Gregory had reported that the Territory's Victoria River had ample water and good pastoral grasslands. James Chambers sent John McDouall Stuart from Adelaide to find more. Stuart, a former employee of the Survey Department and one of Australia's most competent explorers, named the MacDonnell Ranges of central Australia in 1860 in honour of his Governor and continued north toward the sea. He planted the British flag in the geographic centre of the continent and wrote: 'May it be a sign to the natives that the union of liberty, civilisation and Christianity is about to break upon them.' Indeed it was. A few days later Stuart's journey was reversed by indignant Warramunga tribesmen at Attack Creek. He returned the following year but was driven back by the harsh conditions. In 1862 he achieved his ambition of crossing the continent from south to north. On the way he named the Katherine River after the daughter of his patron and Chambers Pillar after the man himself.

The journey was arduous but he saw the Territory during its best seasons and was extravagant in his praise of both the Top End and the central Australian grasslands. In Adelaide he was a hero and the South Australian squatters vociferously demanded the annexation of their neighbour. They wanted the Victoria River region. Governor MacDonnell also expressed a vision that the telegraph line which started in London and finished in India might be extended to the northern coast of Australia and overland to Adelaide. Unlike Stuart's noble hopes for a happy union of cultures, this vision was to become a reality.

South Australia campaigned hard to acquire the Northern Territory. New South Wales did not want to give it up, although it didn't want to use it either. Adelaide politicians presented an astute claim to the British Government which rested largely on Stuart's efforts and the needs of the pastoral industry. On 6 July 1863, their petition was granted. The annexation of the Northern Territory doubled the size of their dominions overnight. The peculiar thing was that nothing substantial happened in the Territory for years. The pastoralists who had cried out for more land were given no immediate leases. The Adelaide politicians who had argued their case turned out to be a government of speculators, not developers. They sold the land in parcels in London and Adelaide, sight unseen, on the principle that the Territory had to pay for itself before anything could be done with it. Most of those who bought the land were also speculators. Cattle and sheep were not driven into the Territory in any great numbers until the 1870s. The focus of government attention was not the original Victoria River region but the far north. An expedition was sent by ship to survey the land parcels which had already been sold. It established a base on the Adelaide River in 1864 but the surrounding land was totally unsuitable and the project was an unmitigated disaster. Its commander was recalled in disgrace and for several years the South Australian Parliament argued about whether it should pay back the land-sale money or press on with settlement and surveys, despite the fact that its legal five years for doing so was finished. It opted for the latter and was lucky to have a most competent man to carry it out.

If John McDouall Stuart was the man who led South Australia into its Northern Territory experiment, George Goyder was the man who saved it from complete collapse. Goyder was the Surveyor-General of South Australia. He had read the explorer's journals and he realised that the deep-water harbour of Port Darwin was the only practical place for a capital before he ever set eyes on it. He arrived there by sea with 120 men in February 1869. The party set up camp on the peninsula which was then occupied by the Larakia Aborigines and which is now the site of Darwin. Goyder recognised the importance of the land to the Aborigines but proceeded with his task. The settlement was to be called Palmerston, after the British Prime Minister. It retained that name for more than forty years. Goyder and his men camped out in the bush and endured the end of the wet season in hammocks. In six months they had surveyed as much surrounding land as their government needed and had laid out the roads of the central townsite. After this prodigious achievement Goyder sailed back to Adelaide.

Palmerston saw out its first year with a few dozen men and a new administrator who was also magistrate, doctor and Protector of Aborigines. The Aborigines continued to live on the land oblivious to the fact that they had been dispossessed by a distant government. None of the Adelaide speculators took up residence on the lands they had bought unsurveyed more than five years before. There was nothing much to do at all. The settlement might have expired, except for a South Australian project which started in October 1870 and which was almost as ambitious as the annexation of the Territory itself. In that month, the colony signed an agreement to build a telegraph line overland from Adelaide to Port Darwin. In return the British Australia Telegraph Company would lay a submarine cable from Java to meet it. This project not only held the key to Australia's future but assured Palmerston's existence and confirmed its strategic importance. The line would one day carry news of the bombing of Darwin to an incredulous nation.

The telegraph line was the catalyst which triggered the development of the Northern Territory. It led to the discovery of gold and the establishment of telegraph repeater stations, many of which became supply points for pastoralists and eventually towns. It helped initiate an era of white settlement which remains unbroken to this day. This era falls naturally into four divisions. The first is the South Australian experiment, characterised by incautious dreams and disenchantment; the second is the bitter period of Commonwealth control and neglect between 1911 and the Second World War; the third is the post-war expansion period under continuing Commonwealth control and the fourth is the period of self-government from 1978 until the present. This last phase is poised to end when the Northern Territory achieves its dream of becoming Australia's seventh State.

The Overland Telegraph Line was completed when two wires were joined at Frew's Pond on 22 August 1872. It stretched more than 3000 kilometres along Stuart's route of exploration from Adelaide to Palmerston. Two months later Australia was in telegraphic communication with England. The days of waiting three months for news by ship had gone forever. The single-wire telegraph had taken two years to string up across some of the most difficult terrain in Australia. It had cost six lives. Construction was supervised by the very capable Charles Todd, Postmaster-General of South Australia. Despite his careful planning, monsoons, swollen rivers and pole-devouring termites made the completion of the northern section extremely difficult. Surveyors named a central Australian waterhole Alice Springs in honour of Todd's wife. A repeater station was built there, as others were at intervals along the line in places like Barrow Creek and Tennant Creek. Linesmen and operators went to live in them and they became little settlements of families, domestic animals and vegetable gardens. South Australia made revenue from charging other colonies for the use of its wonderful new facility. In the Territory the major impact of the telegraph lay in the new grazing areas and minerals discovered during its survey and construction. Two decades of reasonable progress and prosperity lay ahead.

Gold was discovered south of Palmerston at Pine Creek in 1871 and a rush occurred the following year when hundreds of itinerant miners arrived by ship. None of them had anywhere to live, alluvial gold deposits were poor and the big Adelaide companies had already claimed the best reefs. The rush was over within months but extravagant speculation continued unabated for a year or so. A few prospectors stayed on to fossick for gold or to work for the big companies which continued mining around Pine Creek until the turn of the century. The companies imported Chinese labourers from Singapore in 1874 and later from the Kwantung province to work on the goldfields. In 1888, during the construction of the Darwin–Pine Creek railway, the Chinese population in the Top End peaked at seven thousand, outnumbering the Europeans briefly by seven to one before settling back to a four-to-one ratio. Some Chinese stayed to establish their own enterprises in mining, market gardening, fishing and commerce but many returned home after a few years, driven back by loneliness and the ugly racism which grew from white resentment of their industriousness. The Chinese Immigration Act passed through the South Australian Parliament in 1888 and stemmed the Chinese tide. The legislation corresponded to increasing union calls for an 'Australia for Australians'. It reflected the mood of the period leading up to the Commonwealth Government's White Australia Policy of 1901, which stopped Chinese immigration altogether.

Palmerston in those early years was a place of wild men and precious few women. Its population in 1881 was about 3500, of which only 670 were Europeans. Aborigines were not included in the census figures until 1960. The Darwin men were government workers and telegraph employees, company clerks, goldminers, adventurers, drovers, merchants and, within a few years, buffalo shooters and pearl divers. The divers were Malays, Indonesians, Japanese and Filipinos and they added their blood to the racial mixture. Chinatown was in Cavanagh Street, a place of gambling dens, grog shanties and brothels. Drunkenness was a way of life and men lived in hovels. The once happy-go-lucky Larakia Aborigines were pushed out into filthy camps on the fringes of their own peninsula. Men came looking for work from Russia and Eastern Europe. In 1897 a cyclone demolished the shanties and left considerable destruction in its wake. Domesticated buffaloes pulled carts through the streets of Palmerston for the Chinese market gardeners who provided a valuable supply of fresh vegetables.

Early in the 1870s the South Australian Government decided that a transcontinental railway between Adelaide and Palmerston would be the best thing to encourage development in the north. The railway, it was thought, would overcome the Territory's transportation problems altogether. But despite the construction of sections at each end, it was never finished. Between 1886 and 1889 a railway was built by Chinese labourers from Palmerston to Pine Creek to service the goldmining industry. It improved efficiency but the industry was already in decline. After the telegraph was built pastoralists began to move onto the lands sought so eagerly ten years before. The explorers Giles, Warburton and Gosse used camels in the early 1870s to investigate central Australia west of the telegraph and within a few years cattlemen from Queensland were coming in from the east looking for new leases. By the 1880s the Territory had a flourishing pastoral industry in the Victoria River and Barkly Tableland regions. Sheep were tried first but cattle fared better. It was in this decade that the oldest, largest and best-known of Northern Territory cattle stations were established, including Brunette Downs, Wave Hill and Victoria River Downs. The Top End turned out to be useless for grazing animals. It was climatically unsuitable, swampy or stony and its Aborigines killed the white man's cattle. The 1880s were boom years but at the end of the decade came the crash, the speculators' nightmare. Prices and markets crumbled and many of the big companies sold their stations to individual operators at low prices. Recovery was painfully slow.

In 1890 there was a minor goldrush at Arltunga, east of Alice Springs, and this field continued to sustain a small population of diggers for 30 years. The first gold discoveries were made in 1887 and there was increasing pressure from miners and pastoralists for a town to be established. Alice Springs was the local repeater station and the miners and pastoralists had already made it a vital supply depot. The township of Stuart was proclaimed three kilometres south of the repeater station in 1889. Its name was later changed and it became known officially as Alice Springs in 1933. It was like other settlements which sprang up as supply centres for pastoralists: places like Borroloola, far out to the east on the Gulf of Carpentaria, and Katherine, the focus for parts of the Victoria River region. The Territory's first pastoral lease had been taken out at Springvale near Katherine in 1876. The pastoralists of the far Victoria River region drove their cattle to Wyndham in Western Australia, since it was closer. Alice Springs was the natural centre of a large pastoral region and was a vital staging point in the overland route to Tennant Creek and Palmerston. The railway came north from Port Augusta near Adelaide but it stopped at Oodnadatta before it reached the Territory. Drovers took cattle from the Centre to the railhead at Oodnadatta, where the cattle were loaded for southern markets. Out of cattle drives like these came the folklore of the outback.

Camels freighted supplies from the Oodnadatta railhead to Alice Springs and Tennant Creek, another repeater station which had turned into a pastoral depot. Camel trains were flourishing enterprises and their owners imported Afghan

cameleers to drive them. The Afghans, as they were universally called, actually originated from Pakistan. They formed part of the social fabric of the Centre, frequently reviled but always hard-working. Camels had great advantages over horses and bullocks in arid regions and could traverse sandy trackless terrain in scorching heat without drinking water for days, or even weeks. They were first imported for use in inland exploration during the 1860s but, by the end of the century, camel trains had become the essential means of access to Alice Springs. Henry Dutton and Murray Aunger put the writing on the wall for the cameleers when they drove their 25-horsepower, four-cylinder Talbot motor car from Adelaide to Palmerston in 1908 without the benefit of a road. It was the first transcontinental crossing of Australia by car. They pulled the vehicle out of creeks and drove over the lumpy spinifex. The machine looked clumsy but its mechanical shape was undeniably the shape of the future. As motor cars made greater inroads in the 1920s, more and more camels stood idle. When the railway was extended from Oodnadatta to Alice Springs in 1929 the camels were out of a job forever, although the police continued to use them. Huge numbers of camels were sold at low prices or simply released into the wild. The train which replaced them was named 'The Ghan' in memory of their drivers. Most of the Afghans went home.

The first Christian mission in the Territory was set up at Hermannsburg, west of Alice Springs. It was an outpost of the German Lutheran Church established in 1877 by a group of missionaries who took two years to walk there from Bethany in South Australia. Hermannsburg missionaries brought local Aborigines to live at the settlement and in 1891 the first record of the vocabulary and grammar of the Aranda Aborigines was compiled. The acclaimed Aboriginal painter Albert Namatjira was born at Hermannsburg in 1902. Other humanitarian institutions were established after the turn of the century in central Australia. The first nurse was posted to the Inland Mission in 1916 and in 1928 the Mission's Reverend John Flynn established the Royal Flying Doctor Service.

During the early years of northern development, South Australians dreamed of a great agricultural industry in the Northern Territory. Early explorers like Stuart had been deceived by the greenery of the Top End in the wet season and had raved about the region's potential for sugar, cotton, tobacco, rice and other tropical crops. The Government attempted to encourage agricultural enterprises on a grand scale but all such attempts became equally grand failures. Many crops were tried besides those the explorers suggested, including rubber, tea, coffee, peanuts and maize, but the soils were skeletal and impoverished, leached by frequent flooding. A few new industries emerged to fill the gaps left by the ones that failed. In the 1890s wild men began to hunt buffaloes on foot for their hides and they employed Aborigines as trackers and skinners. Joe and Harry Cooper are reputed to have shot 6000 buffaloes on Melville Island in two years from 1895 until Harry was speared to death by the Tiwi people in 1897. The Macassan trepang industry was hounded to its grave by customs duties and licence fees in 1906 but the Europeans showed no inclination to continue it themselves. A pearl shell industry started in 1884 but it was small and economically insignificant.

Telegraph employees, pastoralists and miners all came into conflict with the Aborigines. Many tribes fiercely resisted encroachments on their land. They had no understanding of a system in which their estates could be bought and sold. They killed cattle and sometimes white settlers. In 1874, two telegraph employees at Barrow Creek were speared. In return at least fifty Aborigines were shot in the bush by an Adelaide police party. In 1884 three miners were killed by Aborigines at the Daly River copper mine. Once again a punitive police expedition was organised and mass slaughter ensued. Many pastoralists were humane and protective but others took an aggressive stance and boasted that they shot black men on sight. Aborigines had no racial loyalties except tribal ones and in many cases the new settlers were able to use black against black to their own advantage. The traditional ways of life broke down, despite some conciliation. There was hardly a black person in the whole of Australia's vast inland who had not seen or heard of the white man. Populations were decimated by introduced diseases and whole groups disappeared within a few years. Aboriginal society was also infiltrated by forces which destroyed its health from within, including refined foods and alcohol. Some groups drifted into camps and scavenged for the worst of a new diet. Because they no longer needed to hunt and collect food they abandoned the nomadism which gave their lives its rhythm and meaning. Separated from the traditional lands which linked them to their Dreaming, they descended into spiritual and physical poverty. They were forced to observe two sets of laws or pay the consequences. In 1893, after punitive slaughter started to become distasteful to an increasingly middle-class Australia, an Aboriginal man named Charlie Flanagan became the first person to hang in Palmerston's Fannie Bay Gaol. He was convicted of killing a white station manager in a card game. White men were never punished in the same way for Aboriginal killings. A generation of half-castes emerged which had no place in either black or white society. In Arnhem Land and on the Tiwi islands, tribal people fared better than those in the pastoral regions. Their lands were unusable in a European sense and they were able to maintain the food sources they had always known in the seas, rivers and swamps of the far north. Eventually the people of the inland realised that spears did not deter the settlers but, rather, enraged them, leading to brutal retribution. Many Aborigines consequently went to work for the station managers and became indispensable to them.

The Government of South Australia became increasingly disillusioned by its burdensome northern child during the 1890s. By the turn of the century the Territory was costing it well over a hundred thousand pounds a year to maintain, with little return. The economy throughout the region had stagnated and industries needed massive injections of capital if they were to survive. When South Australia joined forces with the other mainland colonies and Tasmania to establish the Commonwealth of Australia in 1901, it saw its chance to be rid of the problem. It harangued the new Federal Government to take over the Territory with an intensity matching its earlier zeal for annexation. Its efforts were rewarded on 1 January 1911, when the Commonwealth took control following the enactment of the Northern Territory Acceptance Act. The Commonwealth inherited a public debt of four million pounds and a dependent territory in which pastoralism represented the only resilient industry. The population of Palmerston had dropped to less than a thousand people. In 1891 it had been almost five thousand. The name of the northern capital was changed to Darwin in March 1911 and the people of the Territory celebrated the good luck which had seen them delivered from South Australian disenchantment. In fact the Commonwealth was to be far worse. Ominously, it began by depriving Territorians of all political representation.

The Commonwealth Government gave a commitment to complete the transcontinental railway and plans were laid to revitalise the Territory's ailing mining industry. Ambitious new agricultural projects were established at Batchelor and Daly River south of Darwin but they immediately struck the same problems which others had encountered previously. The crops failed repeatedly and in 1918 the projects were abandoned. The Vestey Company of London, which operated in China, Argentina, Russia and France and held the largest area of pastoral land in Australia, built an enormous meatworks on Darwin's Bullocky Point in 1917. At the same time the railway was extended south to the pastoral town of Katherine and men flocked to work in the north. The meatworks employed 500 men and caused the population of Darwin to double within a few years. It was the pillar of the Darwin economy. Employees earned high wages and the works spawned countless peripheral enterprises. But in 1920 the Vestey Company abruptly decided to close the meatworks, claiming that unreliable shipping services and Government delays in extending the railway were endangering the profitability of meat exports. The Darwin economy collapsed as soon as the workers were laid off. Two-thirds of the men in the town were unemployed and there was distress in every quarter. Darwin was a place of inadequate housing and infrastructure. It was dirty and run down; it bred bitterness and frustration.

The Commonwealth Administrator, Dr John Gilruth, had arrived in 1912 and had soon become the most unpopular man in Darwin. His high-handed manner and perceived lack of sympathy fostered resentment. When he closed many of the Territory's hotels and saloons he generated fury in the community. The Darwin Rebellion occurred on 17 December 1918. An angry mob of union men marched to the Government Residence and demanded the Administrator's resignation. They burnt an effigy of Gilruth on the lawn outside in a fraternal outpouring of detestation. Gilruth was defiant to the last but by February 1919 he had been replaced. The problems remained. When the next Administrator came he found a union-run town, a place of transient public and company officials, of wild men and fortune-seekers. The population was a multicultural mixture of Britons, Russians, Eastern Europeans, Greeks, South Americans, Spaniards, Aborigines and Chinamen. Many of the Chinese who had stayed on through the difficult period leading up to the adoption of the White Australia Policy in 1901 and beyond had become successful merchants and market gardeners.

The Aborigines and the Europeans had at least learned to be a little more understanding of their different cultures. There were still no sealed roads to the south and the isolation bore heavily on the nerves of the population, especially during the relentless, oppressive humidity of the wet season build-up. As one person observed, it was a town where some were paid to stay but others had no money to go. Because of its pervading squalor and its frequent and acrimonious industrial disputes, southern newspapers referred to 'Darwin the Damned' and the 'Last Resort of the Australian Derelict'.

Ross and Keith Smith landed in Darwin in 1919 after the first historic flight from England to Australia and Amy Johnson arrived in 1930. The first regular air service between Britain and Australia was established in 1934 and came through Darwin. The isolation paled a little. The railway was extended further south to Birdum in the late 1920s but there it stayed, as the Depression choked the supply of Commonwealth funds. Southern States complained continually of the money wasted on the north. It became painfully obvious that the rest of Australia did not care a fig for the Territory. In the south, the railway was extended from Oodnadatta to Alice Springs in 1929 and the first tourists came the following year. The outback character of Alice Springs charmed the Australian imagination in a way that

Darwin's unruliness did not. The railway proved to be the making of the dusty little town. The new railhead became a point for the loading of cattle and the unloading of freight bound for Darwin. In the late 1930s Eddie Connellan developed his pioneering airline business in and around Alice Springs. The Alice, as it was affectionately known, had a population of 950 people in 1939.

The Depression of the 1930s added to the Territory's economic nightmares. But there was one place which boomed during the Depression decade. This was Tennant Creek, site of Australia's last genuine goldrush. Gold was discovered before the turn of the century but forgotten. In 1930 it was discovered again and in 1933 the rush started in earnest. Desperate men got themselves to the goldfields any way they could and soon hundreds of miners became ant-like figures toiling in a remote landscape. Most of the gold lay in quartzite reefs underground. The diggers set to work with dynamite and blasted impressive potholes in the low hills surrounding the town. The Tennant Creek township grew near a watercourse named by John McDouall Stuart in 1860 and which was initially the site for a telegraph repeater station. There is an old tale that the town acquired its location when a beer and supply wagon broke down a few kilometres short of the repeater station. As legend has it, the miners moved to the wagon and made their town there, rather than cart the supplies back to the creek. This story has been repeated so often it has become folklore. Big companies eventually moved into Tennant Creek but today there are still some solitary diggers blasting through the rock. A large company took over the rich Noble's Nob claim in 1966 and turned it into an open-cut mine. The enormous Warrego gold and copper mine was set up in 1971. Tennant Creek is now a town of about four thousand people. An abattoir was built there in 1980 to service surrounding pastoral leases.

Several church missions were established in Arnhem Land and on the northern islands after the turn of the century. Catholic priests ventured to the islands of the fiercely independent Tiwi people in 1907 and established a church mission which dominated Tiwi lives for seventy years. The Tiwi people achieved self-management in 1978. In the 1880s Paddy Cahill shot buffaloes in Arnhem Land and started an Aboriginal station near Oenpelli. He also started a dairy there in 1906 and ten years later Gilruth's administration bought it during a short-lived enthusiasm for dairy farming. The administration sold it to the Anglican Church Missionary Society in 1925 and it became a mission. In 1931 a huge Aboriginal reserve was declared, covering the entire north-east corner of the Territory. It took the name Flinders had given the north coast: Arnhem Land. By the 1930s it had become apparent the Aboriginal race was not dying out, as early governments had assumed.

In fact numbers had stabilised after the initial decimation and were on the rise. A change of government policy was required. It found its form in assimilation. This new concept was formulated before the war but not implemented until after. It was based on the idea that half-castes could be merged into white society so that their descendants became white. It was well intentioned but presumptuous. Half-caste children were taken from their mothers in one of the most heart-rending episodes in Australian history. Young Aboriginal men were trained to work on stations and girls were trained for domestic service. At some stations the young men were treated like the lowest serfs in a feudal hierarchy, at others they worked in kindly patriarchal systems. They were not paid wages but food, clothes and tobacco. They could not vote because they were not Australian citizens and alcohol was prohibited to them by law. The missions were part of a bygone era in race relations, though they continued to carry out their charitable work and Christian teaching until the 1970s. After the war, large government settlements were built, which took no account of tribal differences but which instead enforced the policies of assimilation.

As the Second World War loomed, military commanders began to take considerable interest in the north. Beyond it lay the threat. The Territory's basic infrastructure had been neglected and its economy left stagnating once more. A small garrison was established in 1936 but it was pitifully insignificant. Work started on a Darwin air base in 1938 and it was still being built when the war started. Australian and American troops moved into the north and non-essential civilians were moved out. On the morning of 19 February 1942, a squadron of 188 Japanese planes arrived to enact a type of Pearl Harbour raid on Port Darwin. Despite the difference in scale it was a watershed for Australians, who had never been attacked on their home soil before. Father John McGrath radioed Darwin within minutes of sighting the planes over Bathurst Island but his message went unheeded for at least 20 minutes. The system of military communication in Darwin was a mess and the raiders arrived before the RAAF could get off the ground. Ten courageous American P40 fighter pilots were the only resistance. Eight ships were sunk and eleven damaged in Darwin Harbour. Planes were destroyed on the airstrip. A bomb went through the roof of the post office, killing eleven people, and another hit the postmaster and his family as they sheltered in a nearby trench. Other bombs were dropped on the hospital at Larrakeyah, near central Darwin. Complacency was cast aside as people dived into the slit trenches they had dug unwillingly only weeks before. In all, 243 people were killed that morning. There was ensuing panic as people began to contemplate an enemy invasion. Many soldiers disappeared into the bush. In retrospect, leadership was found to be lacking but nevertheless there were many heroic actions among the rank and file.

All remaining citizens were evacuated from Darwin to billets in central and southern Australia. Military headquarters moved to Alice Springs where General Douglas MacArthur later stationed himself. The Aborigines were left behind. They were rounded up into work camps and paid wages. The Government was afraid they would collaborate with the Japanese in the event of an invasion. When the Japanese leader of the first raid crashed on Melville Island, however, Matthias Ulungura disarmed him and escorted him all the way to Bathurst Island as a prisoner. The raids on Darwin and the north coast continued and there were sixty-three altogether during 1942 and 1943. The number of American troops in the Territory jumped dramatically. There were at least a hundred thousand military personnel in the Territory during the remainder of the war. The need for a proper road from south to north finally became too pressing to be delayed any longer and the Americans helped build and bituminise the Stuart Highway in 1943. Emergency airstrips were installed alongside it all the way from Darwin to Katherine. For the first time Darwin had a decent road-rail connection to Adelaide and was not totally dependent on shipping for supplies. The Barkly Highway was built from Tennant Creek into Queensland at the same time. When the war ended, the wreckage of aircraft lay strewn across the Top End. Civilians returned to pick up the bits and pieces of their homes and their lives. The entire population of the Territory was just five thousand. A period of rebuilding and reassessment began. Attitudes in Canberra would never be quite as complacent again and, in this sense at least, the war had done Territorians a favour.

After the war, Darwin was militarised in a way it had never been before. It became a modern echo of Britain's Fort Dundas settlement. A major RAAF base was established in Darwin in 1945 and air force planes shared the facilities with civilian aircraft, as they do today. The city grew around the base. After the war, the Commonwealth Government designed new immigration policies to bring hundreds of thousands of workers to Australia. Initially, very few found their way to the Territory, owing to Government restrictions on housing development and leases. But after Robert Menzies became Prime Minister in 1949 people from Europe, Greece, Turkey and the Middle East all went north. The increasing population made the Aborigines a minority in their own land. Darwin became a city in 1959. The pastoral industry was in good shape and export markets were opened up in the Philippines. The era of the overlanders disappeared with the long trucks appropriately named road trains, but the isolation of station life was just the same and just as hazardous. Crocodile shooting became a profitable profession in the Top End in the 1950s when skin prices were high but the industry vanished in 1972 when crocodiles were declared a protected species.

Another ambitious agricultural project disintegrated when the Humpty Doo Rice Project near Darwin, which was backed by American money, failed in 1956. It was abandoned a few years later. Mismanagement, buffaloes, magpie geese and salty soil were all negative factors. Two more major agricultural projects failed before 1974. Meanwhile in the Centre, tourism brought a boom, despite the crippling drought which halved cattle numbers in the rainless years between 1959 and 1965. Mining received a boost when a prospector named Jack White found uranium at Rum Jungle in 1949. In 1954 Rum Jungle became Australia's first uranium mine and the hunt was on for other deposits. They were found in the 1970s in the Alligator Rivers region of Kakadu National Park. Big Tennant Creek mines boomed through these decades with further discoveries of gold, copper and bismuth. In 1959 mining overtook the pastoral industry as the Territory's biggest income earner. Iron ore was mined for eight years after 1966 and generated a brief revenue boost. One of the world's largest deposits of manganese was found at Groote Eylandt, a large island off the Territory coast in the Gulf of Carpentaria, and mining started in 1965. Nearby on the Gove Peninsula, similarly rich deposits of bauxite were discovered in the 1950s. Approval to extract the mineral from the Arnhem Land Aboriginal Reserve was finally granted in the late 1960s and led to the creation of the Territory's most isolated town. It was built to accommodate the families of mine and refinery workers and called Nhulunbuy, the Aboriginal name for the hill which overshadows it. It lies on the north-easternmost extremity of Arnhem Land and the only practical ways of getting there are by aircraft from Darwin or by boat. There is a dirt track to Katherine but it is a rough one and permission to use it is required from the local Aboriginal land council.

Gove bauxite led to the first Aboriginal land rights protest in 1963. The Aborigines objected to the proposed resumption of a part of their reserve for mining. In 1968 they presented a petition signed on bark to the Commonwealth Government. Their case was lost in 1971 when a judge found they had no legal right to the land. But by this time a campaign for land rights was well under way in Australia. The land rights movement started in the 1960s, when white opinion began to swing against the policies of assimilation and when Aborigines rediscovered their own unique, if almost buried, culture. In 1966 there was a strike by 200 Gurindji stockmen at Wave Hill Station, south-west of Katherine. The men were objecting to the fact that they were not paid for their labour as white men were, but received food and clothes instead. It soon became apparent that they were also staking a claim for the return of their traditional land. The mood of the times was moving toward self-determination for the Aborigines. As a result of the strike the Pastoral Award of 1966 decreed that Aborigines had to be paid the same as anyone else for doing the same job. This was one of several victories in a chain of events which began with the Aboriginal right to vote in 1962 and Australian citizenship for all Aborigines in 1964. The latter lifted restrictions on cohabitation and alcohol. In 1975, the Gurindji people were granted leasehold title to their traditional estate. The following year the 1976 Aboriginal Land Rights Bill (Northern Territory) passed through Federal Parliament. It was a clumsy and imperfect piece of legislation, leading to some extravagantly unrealistic land claims, but it represented substantial compensation to Aborigines for previous dispossession of their lands. More than a third of the Northern Territory now belongs to Aborigines. In 1978, tribal Aborigines were granted title to Kakadu, which they then leased to the National Parks and Wildlife Service in 1979 under a 99-year agreement. This allowed for the creation of Kakadu National Park, which has since been included on the World Heritage List. Mining royalties from the Ranger uranium project within the Kakadu boundaries are paid into a land council trust for local Aborigines. These funds pay for bilingual schools, the establishment of business enterprises and community services in Aboriginal towns. The same process led in 1985 to the creation of the Uluru National Park, home of Ayers Rock.

Steady if unspectacular economic development occurred in the Territory throughout the fifties, sixties and seventies. No miraculous, vitalising industry emerged to transform its sluggish progress. The purse-strings of capital development funding lay in Canberra and were infrequently loosened. In the early 1970s Alice Springs' population reached 10 000 and Darwin's 40 000. But before daybreak on Christmas Day 1974 came an event which threw Darwin into total disarray. It was the settlement's fourth major cyclone and Australia's worst natural disaster, codenamed Cyclone Tracy. Virtually every structure in the city was destroyed except for strong government offices and old stone buildings. Worst hit were the houses of the new suburbs which had crept steadily around the RAAF base to dominate its northern perimeter. Wind gusts travelling at speeds of more than 270 kilometres an hour tore the city apart. They sucked up sheets of iron and unwrapped Christmas presents. They even picked up refrigerators and hurled them into the darkness. No one can be sure exactly how powerful these wind gusts were because the measuring apparatus broke when its scale reached 217. More than sixty people were killed on land and sea. Electricity was non-existent and tonnes of food rotted in freezers and refrigerators. A serious health risk lay in contaminated water. Emergency status was conferred on the city immediately. People piled aboard planes bound for families and billets in the south. Others streamed down the Stuart Highway to Tennant Creek, Alice Springs and numerous other points where fellow Territorians responded compassionately to their hunger and homelessness. The whole of Australia pitched in to help with billeting and relief funds. Within a week Darwin's population had plummeted to 12 000. But most residents came back as soon as they could. Within six months the population had climbed back to 30 000. For the second time in thirty years, Darwin's residents rebuilt their city. The astonishing speed with which they did it reflected their typical resilience.

The city which has emerged is an attractive, new place. The old architecture was blown all over the countryside and disappeared. There is almost no vestige today of large slabs of Darwin's history. The old city was partly composed of houses on stilts and these had latticed walls to encourage the flow of cooling breezes. The first buildings after the cyclone were made for strength and climatic suitability was hardly considered. Many of the early rebuilding efforts are brick structures

with few windows. They are devoid of tropical flavour. The building styles which followed reflected a return to some of the good ideas of north Australian architecture. Typical Darwin houses are now built on stilts to bring back the breezes. They can withstand immense winds and pressures. Their slatted windows lock tight and they have strong central fortress zones to protect their occupants during cyclones. New building regulations ensure that extravagant numbers of screws keep their roofs on. The lifestyle is naturally tropical, casual and outdoor-oriented, but in many other aspects it is no different from city life down south. Darwin is still an isolated outpost surrounded by intractability but today it talks to the world at the other end of satellite lines and jet flights. Its life revolves in city circles – in commerce, social services and administration. There are a few city-based professions which offer echoes of the frontier days, like helicopter mustering and cultured pearling, but new professions have arrived and taken over. Horticulturists, medical researchers and marketing strategists are disparate members of the new working community. Darwin has theatres and actors, five-star hotels and recreational facilities to satisfy its sporting passions. In 1987 it had 76 000 people, almost half the population of the Northern Territory. Its most recent additions are the Vietnamese refugee people of the 1970s and the Timorese refugees who came after them. There are no shanty grog shops in Darwin now but there are a few old-timers down the track who remember them. Further down the highway beyond the regional limits of the Top End remain the stockmen, prospectors and brown lands of the past. In the Barkly Tablelands, the Victoria River region and the Centre, men still work from dawn to dusk, trying to make a living out of keeping cattle alive.

Alice Springs is almost a match for Darwin's modernity at the other end of the Territory. It saw its old outback character disappear with the coming of new tourism developments but retained its small-town charm, despite its population of more than twenty thousand. It has a busy arts complex, major hotels, restaurants and resorts. It is still an important railhead for the pastoral industry and for Darwin-bound freight. The Territory's other major towns, Katherine, Tennant Creek and Nhulunbuy, each have several thousand residents. In the east, Borroloola has a few hundred and in the west, Timber Creek a few dozen. A succession of roadhouse settlements survive on the trade of the Stuart Highway. In every region there are major Aboriginal communities; places like Papunya and Yuendumu in the Centre, and Milingimbi and Maningrida in Arnhem Land. Some of these communities run their own radio and television stations and others, like Yirrkala and Bathurst Island, sell their art to the world. Throughout the Territory there are small Aboriginal outstations where people have redefined their lives using elements from two cultures. They hunt ancient food sources in Arnhem Land using modern weapons and combine Christian teaching with ceremonial ritual. In 1987, the Territory had 158 000 residents, easily making it the most sparsely populated political region in Australia.

The Northern Territory has experienced unprecedented growth since 1978. In that year the Commonwealth gave the Territory many of the self-determining powers enjoyed by Australian States but retained control of Aboriginal affairs, mining and national parks. In effect the Commonwealth transferred the role of administering the Territory from itself to a new parliament in Darwin. Most funding for Territory expenditure still comes from the Commonwealth but the Darwin

Government is passionate in its search for self-supporting industries, which will add depth to the shallow economic base which has dogged the Territory throughout its short history. Mining is by far the biggest industry at present although it is conducted almost exclusively by firms from interstate or overseas. The other major industries are pastoralism, tourism and fishing and new ones are developing in horticulture and manufacturing. The Darwin administration has been both cautious and daring. It has balanced its budgets and carefully assessed infrastructure needs in order to best direct funds for future expansion. Such an example is the port, which has been given up-to-date roll-on, roll-off loading facilities, for Darwin is still largely reliant on shipping.

The Government dreams of finishing the transcontinental railway first proposed more than a hundred years ago. It hopes a private consortium will build and operate a line from Darwin to Alice Springs. It has already coaxed a consortium to build a 1500-kilometre pipeline from Alice Springs to Darwin. This line now pumps cheap fuel for the new Darwin power station from huge fields of oil and gas in the Amadeus Basin, west of Alice Springs. New housing areas, like Palmerston in Darwin, are expanding at a rate far above the national average. Construction of the first part of the massive Tindal RAAF base at Katherine has turned that little pastoral centre into a boom town. The pastoral industry itself is getting back on its feet after a period in the economic wilderness. It is adapting to new markets for buffalo and horse meat. Live cattle are exported to Malaysia and Brunei and there are many other trade links with the Southeast Asian region, the fastest-expanding economic area in the world. Darwin rightly considers itself an integral part of this region, since it is closer to Kupang and Jakarta than to major Australian capitals.

The Northern Territory Government harbours a long-cherished dream of statehood. Its ambition is to see the Territory take its place beside Australia's six existing States on an equal standing and with the same constitutional rights and responsibilities. The Territory is a place like no other and its future is sure to be as remarkable as its past. Perhaps its political coming of age will open a new and brighter chapter in the story of the Australian Aborigines. The challenge ahead lies in balancing the Dreaming with the budget.

The Photographs

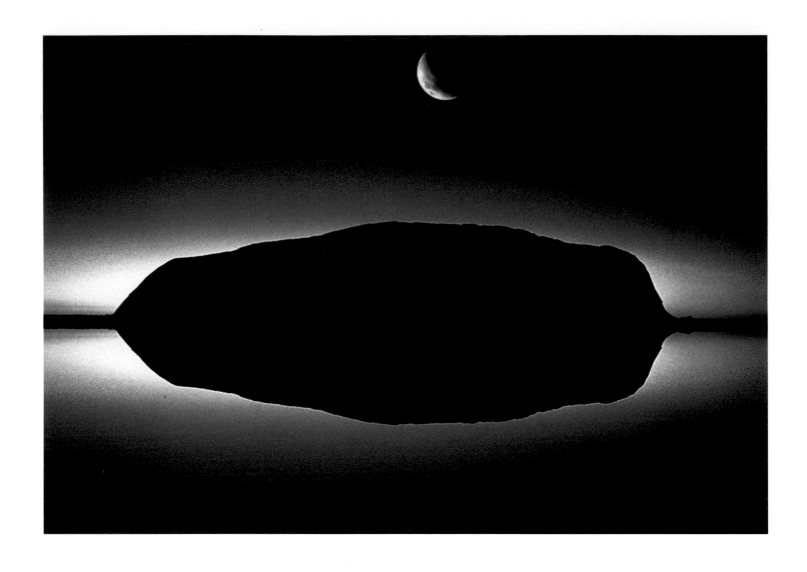

Ayers Rock, a symbol of creation. Every scar, cave and waterhole is significant

Close up, the surface of the Rock is peeling and flaking

In a system with no formal leaders, Aboriginal elders have the highest authority

The X-ray style of Aboriginal painting, depicting internal organs and bones

The Olgas in an orange mood as the sun emerges during a dust storm

Thirty-six domes make up the Olgas, seen here during a storm

The Camel King, Noel Fullerton, learned his skills from the Afghans

Bobby is a tribal Aborigine, as indicated by the ceremonial incisions on his body

The dramatic beginning of the wet season at Tennant Creek

Lightning is a common occurrence in the Top End, and storms are dramatic

One of Australia's most inhospitable regions, the Simpson Desert

The flightless emu thrives in the arid conditions of the Simpson Desert

A joyful smile from a desert woman decorated for a special ceremony

Face paint gives a fearsome look to this man taking part in a burial ceremony.

Brolgas, elegant members of the crane family, gather in large flocks in Kakadu

Paperbarks survive in the Wet when the Magela floodplain becomes a vast lagoon

The comic gait of the frill-necked lizard on the run

Belying its name, the thorny devil is actually the most timid of creatures

Sunset on Mindil Beach, one of Darwin's most popular seaside spots.

Darwin's Mindil Beach is a playground for the many children who live there.

Australia's only stork, the stately jabiru, at Yellow Waters in Kakadu

A pair of jabirus nesting in the highest branches of a tree after the rains

Ugly and dangerous, wild boars are feral descendants of introduced pigs.

Dingoes are hunters and scavengers, capable of killing a kangaroo

Flowers blooming on the Magela floodplain at the end of the wet season

The South Alligator River, mistakenly named after its crocodiles

These water buffaloes are similar in number to those first brought to Australia

The delightful egret wanders alone in search of food in a grassy swamp

Lotus lilies opening their petals in the early morning at Fogg Dam

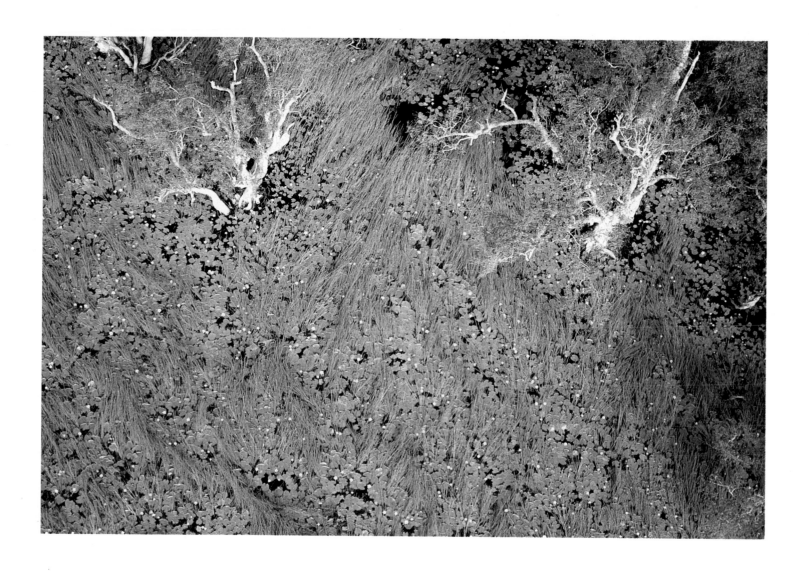

A billabong, almost concealed by water lilies, reeds and paperbark trees

Aborigines have been employed as stockmen on cattle stations since 1879

Even at dawn there's work to be done at Muckaty Station, north of Tennant Creek

A smoko break for a stockman on a central Australian station.

A Tiwi Aborigine from Bathurst Island decorated for a burial ceremony.

Yellow Waters in Kakadu takes its name from these ephemeral flowers

Pelicans flying over the Magela floodplain create a startling pattern

These palms, found nowhere else in the world, thrive in the desert's searing heat

This stone colonnade leads into Arnhem Land's 'Ruined City', a sacred site

The contrast between the wet and dry seasons at Rainbow Valley

A rainbow over Rainbow Valley in a rare communion of namesakes

The Barrow Creek publicans. Barrow Creek is a tiny town north of Alice Springs

To make a deposit at The Creek Bank simply write your name on a banknote

Without a beach umbrella, sunbathers in the Territory can be seriously burnt

It looks like heaven, this beach on the Gove Peninsula in the far north

The fifth canyon of the Katherine Gorges in the Arnhem Land plateau

The desert oak, not the sort of tree you'd expect to find in 40-degree heat

The students of Darwin High School painted this mural on the school wall

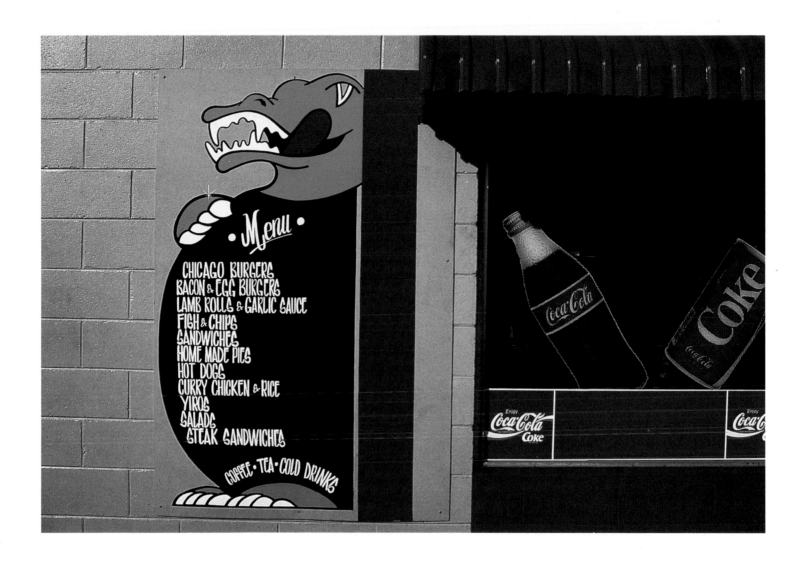

Everything is colourful in Darwin: the sky, the sea and the takeaway shop

In a small reserve lie hundreds of large boulders, the Devil's Marbles

The Aboriginal name for Chambers Pillar means 'place of the adulterous male'

The wet season in Kakadu. A solitary flower blooms among the swamp grasses

An island of red earth surrounded by Lake Amadeus, a mostly dry salt lake

The colours most often associated with the outback: red earth and blue sky

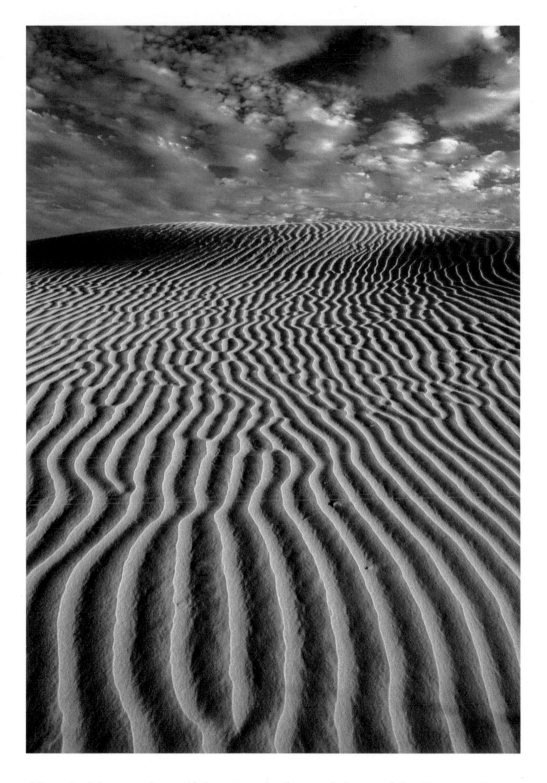

The wind forms a beautiful pattern in the sand dunes of the Simpson Desert

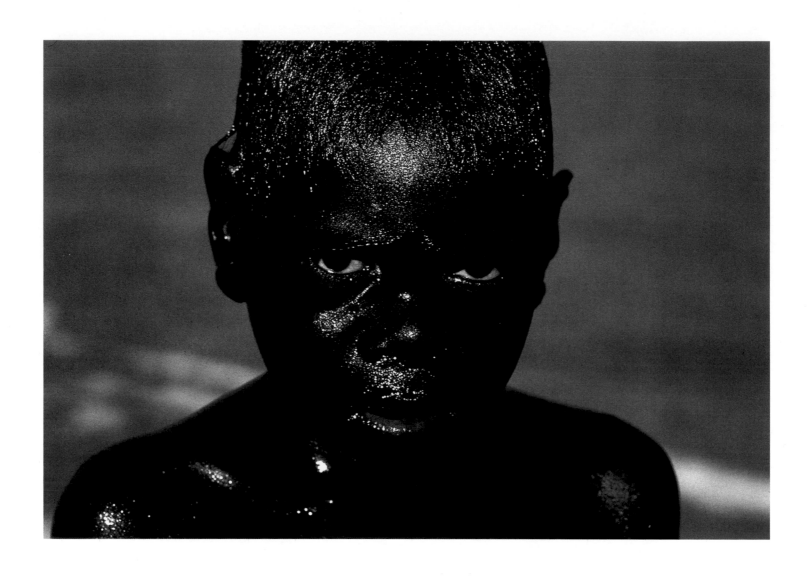

A Tiwi Aboriginal boy from Bathurst Island glistens in the sun after a swim

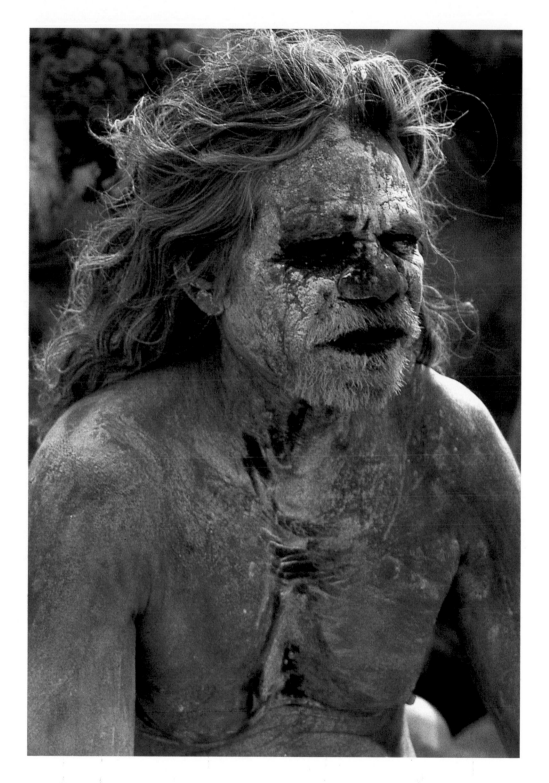

During burial ceremonies white clay is painted on the face and body

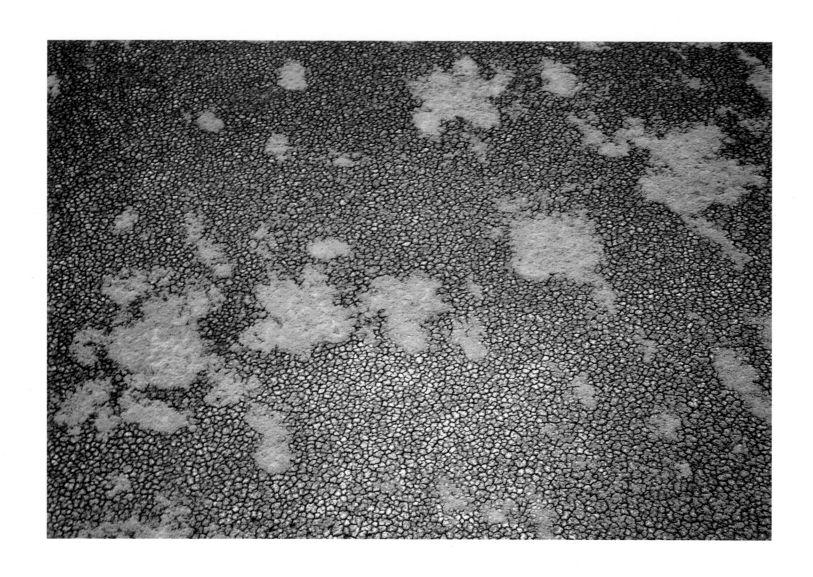

In the dry season in the Top End, practically everything dries up

In the Wet, Top End swamps come to life at an explosive rate

A pair of pelicans seen here at sunrise on the Magela floodplain

This plumed egret has a neat trick for catching fish while standing still

Lotus birds are also called 'Christ birds' because they seem to walk on water

Even in the dry season, Yellow Waters can always sustain the birds

The Diamond Beach Hotel-Casino in Darwin, built in the early 1980s

The Sheraton Hotel at the Yulara Resort with its unique sail-like shades

Race day at Timber Creek and a young boy is dressed for the big event

From the verandah of the Barrow Creek Hotel you can see just about everything

Windmills pump water from artesian basins into great elevated storage tanks

Sunset in central Australia. Softer and more subtle than those of the north

As the dry season wears on, the surface of a claypan dries and contracts

Reflections in a rock pool at the base of King's Canyon

In this central Australian ceremony, leaves are tied into rustling anklets

Children frolicking in the surf at Bathurst Island, north of Darwin

A rare and beautiful sight: Ayers Rock in a blue mood streaked with silver

All Australians feel the urge to visit Ayers Rock sooner or later

The gold nugget discovered by Ray and Maria Hall at the Kurrinilly Mine

Prospectors Ray and Maria Hall stand jubilantly at their diggings

The breaking of a new day reveals another aspect of Yellow Waters

A solitary darter seen here at first light at Yellow Waters in Kakadu

Students and teachers from Darwin's multicultural Parap Primary School

One of several murals in Darwin painted by the students of the High School

The distinctive sails of the Yulara Sheraton Hotel on a still, clear night

Modern technology seems out of place against this magnificent sunset

A magpie goose shakes the water from its only partially webbed feet

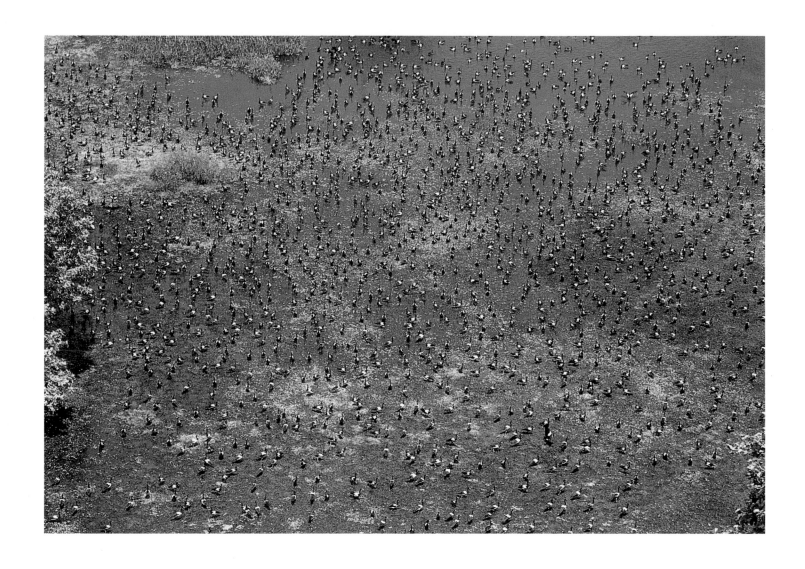

Magpie geese spread out over the floodplains to breed during the Wet

Early morning training along the dry bed of the Todd River in Alice Springs

A jockey's polished boots and dazzling breeches at the Darwin Turf Club

The Mindil Beach Weekend Market is one of several such markets in Darwin

Chebasio Gima from the Kuni tribe of New Guinea is a pearl diver in Darwin

Paragliding and other water sports are restricted to the dry season

This unusual opaque green water is the shallow Arafura Sea

Every member of the clan is involved in a corroboree, even young children

Darwin's German community celebrates St Martin's Day each year

Darwin at night. From a frontier town to a thriving commercial centre

Timorese refugees, now residents of Darwin, pose by the Timor Sea

Since their introduction, wild buffaloes have caused havoc in the Territory

Perfectly camouflaged, a saltwater croc lurks among the mangroves

A water dragon keeps a wary look-out beside a watercourse in the Top End

The rare Oenpelli python, identified in 1977 by Graeme Gow

Fun and games on a waterfall on the Arnhem Land escarpment

This rock pool is created by rainwater draining off the Arnhem Land escarpment

One of the most beautiful ways to see central Australia – in a hot-air balloon

The red Alice Springs racetrack. Racing is a popular sport in the Territory

These strange-looking pillars are the homes of millions of termites

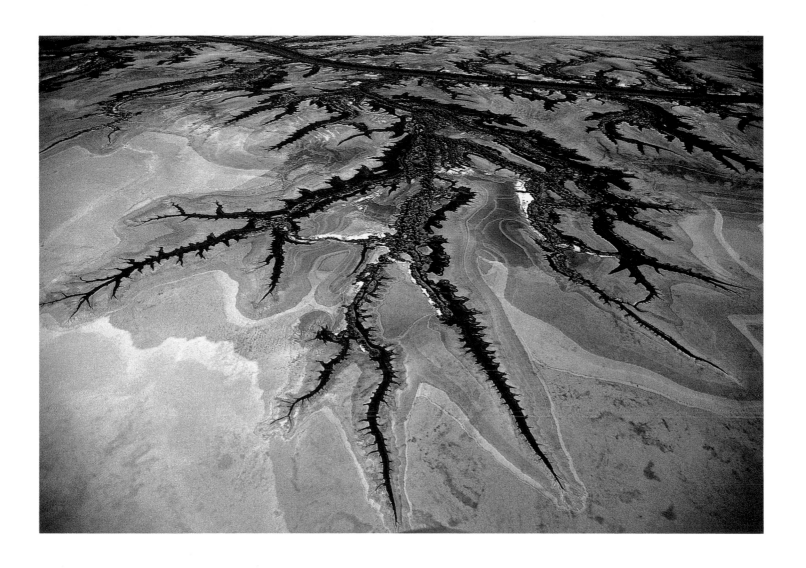

These are called dendritic drainage patterns, left when the tide goes out

Picture Captions

1 Mystical and awe-inspiring, Ayers Rock rose from the flat landscape left by a vast inland sea millions of years ago. The Pitjantjatjara Aborigines believe that during the Dreamtime of creation, Ayers Rock was a low sandhill with a waterhole on it. They called it Uluru. It was inhabited by the great Rainbow Serpent spirit, a terrifying creature as long and colourful as a rainbow. When the Dreamtime ended, Uluru became a gigantic rock, inhabited still by the fearful snake spirit. The Rock is sacred, a symbol of creation itself, and every scar, cave and waterhole has its origin in the Dreamtime. In 1985, the Australian Government handed control of Uluru back to its traditional custodians, the Pitjantjatjara people.

First image taken approximately 20 minutes before sunrise, with the only visible light directly behind Ayers Rock. 35 mm Rokkor lens, f:5.6/8 1 sec. The image was then flipped and the moon added later to create a more realistic sky. This gives the impression of a giant pool of water in front of Ayers Rock. The unusual colour is quite common in the early mornings of central Australia. The image was created in the camera and no filters were used. Pin registration is very important. Kodachrome 25 ASA Pro. Photo for advertising use.

2 The surfaces of Ayers Rock near its base show evidence of the rust-like flaking which has been slowly eroding the great red monolith for aeons. The Rock is made of sandstone strata and erosion along these layers has created its massive ridges. It was thrust up at an 85-degree angle about 450 million years ago and it has been worn smooth by time. The Rock rises 335 metres above the plain and is 2.5 kilometres long, 1.5 kilometres wide and 9 kilometres in circumference. Lying about 350 kilometres south-west of Alice Springs, it was named by the explorer William Gosse in 1873 in honour of the Premier of South Australia at the time, Sir Henry Ayers.

200 mm Rokkor lens, f:5.6 Kodachrome 64 ASA.

3 An Aboriginal elder belonging to a desert tribe of central Australia stands before Ayers Rock, the apotheosis of his Dreamtime mythology. In a communal system which generally has no need of formal leaders, elders have the highest authority. Of all the members of the clan, they have the deepest understanding of tribal traditions and beliefs. After initiation as boys of 12 to 14 years, young Aboriginal men start a long process of instruction in tribal law and customs which continues throughout their lives. In central Australia, where survival is more difficult than in the north, initiated men perform secret rituals to ensure the continuation of food species.

135 mm Rokkor lens, f:5.6 1/30 sec. Kodachrome 25 ASA.

4 Using white clay as paint and the frayed end of a reed as a brush, an Aborigine from Oenpelli paints a design on a rock face in the traditional way of his ancestors. The Arnhem Land escarpment at Oenpelli is rich in cave paintings, some of them dating back more than 18 000 years. On nearby Obiri Rock there are paintings of the Tasmanian tiger, now extinct on the Australian mainland. Anthropologists have found that these paintings mirror changing Aboriginal food sources over the centuries. At Obiri there are the fluid 'mimi' figures of an early period and a gallery of fish painted in the famous X-ray style, which depicts internal organs and bones.

28–85 mm zoom Rokkor lens, f:8 1/15 sec. Kodachrome 64 ASA.

5 The Olgas appear bathed in the diffused golden light of a rainbow as the sun emerges during a storm. Both the Olgas and Ayers Rock were formed about 450 million years ago when an enormous upheaval pushed parts of the earth's stratified crust up through the ground. The Olgas emerged at an angle of about 20 degrees as craggy outcrops but rain and wind have long since smoothed them into rounded domes. The explorer Ernest Giles called them 'monstrous pink haystacks' when he saw them in 1872. The Olgas, 32 kilometres from Ayers Rock, exude a certain unearthliness which touches visitors with awe.

When I arrived at the Olgas the sky was overcast. I spotted a gap of blue sky to the west and waited three-quarters of an hour for the sun to break through, as I realised this would throw the late afternoon sunlight directly onto the Olgas. At the very moment the sun appeared it began to drizzle with rain, generating a rainbow. The scene held for three minutes before the sun disappeared behind the cloud cover once again.

20 mm, f:8 1/60 sec. Kodachrome 64 ASA.

6 The thirty-six domes of the Olgas glow red, as a desert dust storm envelops and reflects the last rays of the sun. The Olgas have always been overshadowed by nearby Ayers Rock but are just as important in the mythology of Pitjantjatjara Aborigines, who call them Katajuta, meaning 'many heads'. The domes cover 65 square kilometres and are a composite of granite, basalt and other rocks, cemented by fine sandstone. The largest dome is Mount Olga, which stands 450 metres above the surrounding plain. It was named in 1872 in honour of Queen Olga of Württemberg by the explorer Ernest Giles.

600 mm APO Rokkor lens, f:8 tripod, photographed from approximately 20 km away.

7 Noel Fullerton, commonly known as the 'Camel King', lives near Alice Springs and has been handling camels for nearly twenty years. Noel used to drive road trains through the Territory but these days leads camel safaris to places where few white people have ever been, through some of the most inaccessible country in central Australia. Noel says he learnt a great deal by talking to Afghans, who came with the first camels to Australia in the latter part of the last century. The Alice Springs Camel Cup originated as a bet betweeen Noel and a friend more than fifteen years ago and is now an annual event. Noel says after he'd suffered three consecutive defeats in the Cup, the Afghans taught him how to catch and breed the fastest camels in the land.

200 mm Rokkor lens, f:5.6/8 1/60 sec. Kodachrome 64 ASA.

8 Bobby is a traditional tribal Aborigine, as indicated by the ceremonial incisions on his arms and body. He lives in Arnhem Land at Oenpelli, home of the Gunwinggu people. On the day this photograph was taken, he was setting out to hunt magpie geese with his shotgun – a new weapon for an old target when considered in the context of the Aborigines' 40 000-year inhabitation of Arnhem Land. Despite his avowed age of sixty-five, Bobby is as agile as a wallaby. He is an exceptional tracker and hunts game in Kakadu during the year to supply his needs just as his ancestors did. (Visitors are not allowed to bring firearms into the park.) Bobby is also a renowned painter, one of the best in Oenpelli.

200 mm Rokkor lens, f:5.6/8 1/60 sec. Kodachrome 64 ASA.

9 The first rainstorm of the wet season near Tennant Creek. Towering, flat-bottomed thunderclouds roll down from the north and dump an average of 300 millimetres of water a year on the southern part of the Barkly Tablelands. The landscape around Tennant Creek, 964 kilometres south of Darwin, is one of semi-arid plains clothed in spinifex and mulga, punctuated by low rocky hills. The Warramunga Aborigines lived in the area before European settlement and fiercely resisted encroachments upon their territory. John McDouall Stuart was turned back by hostile Warramunga warriors at Attack Creek during his attempt to traverse the continent from south to north in 1860.

300 mm Rokkor lens, f:5.6 1/15 sec., tripod. Ektachrome 64 ASA.

10 The first lightning of the northern wet season explodes out of a fulminating ceiling of black cloud. More lightning cracks over Darwin and nearby Melville Island each year than any other place in the country. The city averages more than eighty days of thunder activity during summer, and with the storms comes torrential tropical rain. The transformation in the landscape is sudden and extreme. The cracked soil turns to mud, then becomes swamp covered with bursting growth. The Wet arrives in November and continues until March. The winter Dry lasts from May until September. The Top End is prone to violent tropical cyclones in the wet season.

This photograph is a combination (in camera) of two images to dramatise the change in season from the Dry to the start of the Wet. Lightning: 135 mm Rokkor lens, f:5.6, shutter at B. Cracked soil: 20 mm Rokkor lens, f:11 1/30 sec. Kodachrome 25 ASA.

11 The Simpson Desert, probably the most inhospitable region in Australia, covers an area of 170 000 square kilometres – about three-quarters the size of Victoria. A large part of it is situated in the south-east corner of the Northern Territory. Despite the Sahara-like appearance of these sand dunes near the Queensland border, the Simpson Desert's terrain and vegetation are surprisingly diverse. It is dominated by thousands of parallel sand ridges, about 400 metres apart, running for hundreds of kilometres in a NNW-SSE direction.

28–85 mm zoom Rokkor lens, f:11 1/30 sec. Kodachrome 64 ASA.

12 The Simpson Desert may be desolate but it is not by any means a continental 'dead heart', as it was once labelled. Australia's giant flightless bird, the emu, survives in the desert on insects and grasses. The emu resembles the ostrich but is smaller and has a feathered head and neck as well as rudimentary wings. It is found throughout Australia but generally inhabits more verdant coastal areas. The emu lives in pairs or groups on the Simpson's sandy plains, where it builds ill-concealed grass nests for its eggs. The male sits on the eggs for about eight weeks and waits for the offspring to hatch.

200 mm Rokkor lens, f:5.6 Kodachrome 64 ASA.

13 An Aboriginal desert woman of central Australia is decorated in white clay and red and yellow ochres for a special ceremony. The body paint represents the woman's tribal totem. Aboriginal women conduct rituals forbidden to men and also take an active and enthusiastic part in the dancing and singing during general corroborees. They contribute to the music by beating together sticks or boomerangs. The explorer John Eyre witnessed many Aboriginal corroborees during his travels in the interior. He described the character of the dances as 'grossly licentious' but nevertheless said he found them beautiful and moving.

28–85 mm zoom Rokkor lens, f:5.6 Kodachrome 25 ASA. Last daylight.

14 An Aboriginal man from the Roper River region of southern Arnhem Land is steeped in the mythology of his clan as he takes part in a tribal burial ceremony. The face paint is part of a symbolic ritual which connects the mourner to his totem, or mythic spiritual being. Complex mortuary rites convey the dead person's spirit back to the intangible dimension of the Dreaming, where immortality is guaranteed. Aboriginal burial ceremonies differ throughout the Territory according to the totemic legends of each tribal group. The death of an important member of a tribe will draw grieving kinspeople from a wide radius to the burial ceremony.

200 mm Rokkor lens, f:5.6 1/60 sec. available light Kodachrome 64 ASA.

15 Brolgas wade across a coastal floodplain in the Top End. The brolga is a member of the crane family and is found throughout northern Australia. Inevitably, large flocks find their way to Kakadu, where food in the form of insects, frogs, reptiles and vegetation is easier to find than in other regions during the dry season. Brolgas in flight are a graceful spectacle but they have comical courtship rituals. They leap, bow and prance with exaggerated steps, honking their trumpeting call. They breed during the wet season and build their nests in swamps.

Aerial – 28–85 mm zoom Rokkor lens, f:5.6 1/125 sec. Ektachrome 64 ASA.

16 During the wet season the Magela floodplain in Kakadu National Park becomes a vast lagoon covering hundreds of square kilometres. Some areas are dotted with paperbark trees as here, while others are dominated by thick reeds or watery carpets of lilies. Thousands of blundering wild buffaloes almost destroyed the freshwater ecology of this landscape in the late 1960s and early 1970s by eroding a channel to the East Alligator River and allowing salt water to pour into the lagoon. Rangers closed the channel and the delicate environment began to rejuvenate itself. All the buffaloes have now been removed from the park.

Aerial – 28–85 mm zoom Rokkor lens, f:5.6 1/125 sec. Ektachrome 64 ASA.

17 This is the upper part of Twin Falls, one of Kakadu's three major waterfalls on the Arnhem Land escarpment. A little further down, the water reaches a point where it simply hurtles over the edge of a tall cliff to crash noisily into the gorge below. In the wet season, when the raging torrents are at their most ferocious, the spray can soak a person standing hundreds of metres down the gorge. Twin Falls and its equally impressive neighbour, Jim Jim Falls, drain into Jim Jim Creek, a tributary of the South Alligator River. The brute force of the rainstorms which generate these waterfalls has to be seen to be believed. The rain doesn't just fall – it drives down mercilessly.

28–85 mm zoom Rokkor lens, f:8 1/125 sec. Kodachrome 64 ASA.

18 Rainbow Valley lies 120 kilometres south of Alice Springs on Orange Creek Station. Its dramatic outcrops have names like 'Mushroom Rock' and 'Lion's Head' but they have none of the rounded smoothness of Ayers Rock, the Olgas and the Devil's Marbles. The patchy red colouring is a result of the oxidation of iron deposits suspended in sedimentary sandstone. These striking red outcrops, especially when contrasted with the vivid blue of a desert sky, are among the Territory's most photogenic sights.

200 mm Rokkor lens, f:5.6 Kodachrome 25 ASA. Late afternoon.

19 A frill-necked lizard, evidently alarmed, runs on its hind legs using its tail for balance. When it gets moving, the lizard's gait resembles a person pedalling a bicycle. Found throughout Kakadu and northern Australia, the frill-necked lizard can grow to a metre in length. It spends much of its time in trees out of harm's way and ventures down to hunt for ants, spiders and small mammals. The lizard's most interesting feature is a brightly coloured ruff of skin, normally folded behind its neck, which it puts up like an umbrella when cornered or threatened. When the frill goes up, the lizard opens its mouth to reveal a bright-yellow interior, a combination designed to completely terrify its aggressor.

200 mm Rokkor lens, f:5.6 1/125 sec. Kodachrome 64 ASA.

20 The thorny devil, *Moloch horridus*, may look a fearsome creature but it is the epitome of timidity. Its nasty-looking spikes are soft and its jaws weak. It lives on a diet of ants and can consume as many as 6000 in one meal with its speedy tongue. Found in desert regions of central Australia, the 20-centimetre thorny devil spends most of its time under logs and bushes, venturing out only to look for food. One thorny devil was reported by a naturalist as having moved just 13 metres in three days. Thorny devils are extremely delicate and every attempt to keep them in captivity has failed, owing to their specialised diet.

50 mm macro Rokkor lens, f:8 1/15 sec. Kodachrome 25 ASA.

21 The reflection of a boy carrying his empty fishing net shimmers across the golden ripples of a tidal pool on Darwin's Mindil Beach. Behind him lies Beagle Gulf, named after the ship which landed the first European at Port Darwin. That person was Lieutenant John Lort Stokes, who named the site Port Darwin in 1839 in honour of Charles Darwin, a young naturalist who had sailed aboard the *Beagle* on an earlier voyage. Beyond Beagle Gulf lies the Timor Sea and Timor itself, 600 kilometres away. Mindil Beach is one of Darwin's most popular seaside spots. It is three kilometres from the city centre and is framed at either end by craggy headlands.

135 mm Rokkor lens, f:8 1/500 sec. Kodachrome 25 ASA.

22 A young girl wearing a bright headdress plays in the sand at Mindil Beach. Compared with other Australian cities, Darwin's population is youthful. In the past, when the Territory was administered by South Australia and later the Commonwealth, government workers returned south once their period of duty in the north was over, making way for new workers with young families who would also stay for a few years. A large transient population has always been a permanent characteristic of the city. This still occurs to a certain extent and there is a relatively small retired community. But things are changing. Substantial numbers of migrants from Southeast Asia have made homes in the city, and, as Darwin becomes larger and more modernised, more Australians want to live there permanently.

28–85 mm Rokkor lens, f:8 1/125 sec. Kodachrome 25 ASA.

23 The stately jabiru, the prince of all the birds found in Kakadu and Australia's only stork, stands in the shallows at Yellow Waters keeping a sharp eye out for freshwater crustaceans and fish. When it sees food, the jabiru lunges with its huge bill. It is also called the black-necked stork, after the markings which distinguish it from European species, but 'jabiru' is the favoured name in the Top End. The word comes from the Tupi language of South America, where it is the name for another species of stork. The most startling aspects of the jabiru are its considerable size, its long, bright orange legs, its piercing eyes and its bold symmetrical black-and-white markings.

200 mm Rokkor lens, f:8 1/60 sec. Kodachrome 25 ASA.

24 A pair of jabirus nesting in the highest branches of a tree in an area near the Adelaide River floodplain, not far from Darwin. The distinguishing feature between male and female jabirus is the colour of their eyes. The female's are an intense yellow while the male's are dark. The birds breed and build their nests out of harm's way after the heavy rains. They weave sticks and twigs into the branches of low swamp trees or higher woodland trees and overlay this structure with grass or rushes. Their low, heavy flight is a graceful spectacle and they are quite easily seen by visitors to Kakadu.

Aerial – 28–85 mm zoom Rokkor lens, f:5.6 1/60 sec. Kodachrome 25 ASA.

25 Like so many other animals in the Northern Territory, the wild boars of the Top End are the feral descendants of a species introduced to Australia by Europeans. They have thrived in the tropical north where there is always water to drink and plenty of vegetation to eat. And, like the buffaloes and wild horses, they have disturbed the delicate natural balance of an environment which never had a place for them.

Aerial – 28–85 zoom Rokkor lens, f:11 1/30 sec. Kodachrome 64 ASA.

26 A dingo runs from the clatter of a helicopter in the Top End. The dingo is a wild dog found throughout the Territory and the rest of mainland Australia. It is generally agreed that it came to Australia from the north with the Aborigines. Excavated remains show that the dingo has lived in Australia for at least 8000 years. It once ranged in colour from pale yellow to black, while some were multi-coloured, but is now most commonly yellow with white markings. The dingo is a hunter and scavenger and is quite capable of killing a kangaroo. It is often seen on the rocky outcrops of central Australia.

Aerial – 28–85 mm zoom Rokkor lens, f:11 1/15 sec. Kodachrome 25 ASA.

27 Spindly trees and a carpet of tiny yellow flowers provide yet another example of the rich diversity of the Magela floodplains. The flowers bloom at the end of the wet season for a very short time. To the Aborigines, who were aware of every changing nuance of the landscape, little things like this were part of a tapestry of occurrences which mapped out their six seasons. A small natural event indicated the time was right to dig for a particular wild vegetable, look for a particular fruit or anticipate the return of a particular fish or bird. The waters on the vast Magela plains remain for up to nine months of the year and in a few places they are permanent.

135 mm Rokkor lens, f:5.6 Ektachrome 64 ASA.

28 The great South Alligator River floodplains lie in the western part of Kakadu National Park. The river starts on the Arnhem Land plateau and winds through the park to the Van Diemen Gulf, its volume multiplied by countless tributaries in the wet season. In fact, there are no alligators in the river or in Australia. The thousands of saltwater crocodiles which inhabit the South Alligator River were mistakenly identified by the commander of the HMS *Mermaid*, Phillip Parker King, who undertook survey work on the north Australian coast in 1818. King also named the East Alligator River for the same reason.

20 mm Rokkor lens, f:8 1/15 sec. Kodachrome 25 ASA.

29 This herd of water buffaloes moving across a floodplain on the Cobourg Peninsula is almost identical in number to the first group of beasts brought to mainland Australia in 1827. They were imported to the Cobourg Peninsula from Southeast Asia to provide agricultural aid for the first European settlements in the Territory. When the settlements failed, the buffaloes ran wild. They adapted superbly to the wetland environment of Kakadu and by 1981 their numbers had swelled to almost 300 000. Little did the early settlers realise the enormous damage that these creatures would eventually do to the fragile ecology of the Top End.

Aerial – 28–85 mm zoom Rokkor lens, f:5.6 Ektachrome 64 ASA.

30 A large egret wades in a swamp-grass haven of the Top End. Large egrets are common in the wetland areas of the north and may be seen as close to Darwin as Fogg Dam, an hour's drive from the city. Large egrets are most often seen alone, watching and probing for the fish, frogs and aquatic insects that inhabit swamps and the margins of rivers and streams. Fogg Dam is a permanent waterhole, one of a few, and like the other freshwater billabongs which remain in the dry season, it becomes an increasingly crowded refuge for birdlife as the wetlands gradually disappear.

200 mm Rokkor lens, f:8 1/60 sec. Ektachrome 64 ASA.

31 Lotus lilies start to open their petals to receive the morning sun at Fogg Dam, near Darwin. Fogg Dam is a shallow man-made lake which was established at Humpty Doo on the Adelaide River floodplain in 1954 to irrigate an ambitious rice-growing project. The project, financed largely by American businessmen, failed as a result of inexperience and poor management. It was abandoned in 1960. The dam is now neglected. In the dry season it becomes home to an astonishing variety of wildlife. Delicate lotus birds can be seen trotting across the lily pads while waders stalk their prey among the shallows. The dam is also inhabited by saltwater crocodiles which find access during wet-season flooding.

20 mm Rokkor lens, f:11 1/30 sec. Ektachrome 64 ASA.

32 Water lilies, reeds and paperbark trees shroud the surface of a billabong on the Cobourg Peninsula, north-east of Darwin. Country like this, inaccessible and unusable in any agricultural sense, was regarded as useless by early European visitors to the Top End. To the Aborigines, however, it provided everything needed to sustain life. Three British attempts at settlement failed on the Cobourg Peninsula between 1824 and 1849. These settlements were to have been commercial centres for Britain in the Southeast Asian region, but the trade never came. Those who sent the expeditions badly underestimated the extreme conditions and their effect on the morale of the settlers.

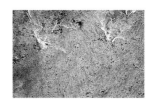

Aerial – 28–85 mm zoom Rokkor lens, f:5.6 1/125 sec. Ektachrome 64 ASA.

33 Aborigines had never seen horses or cattle before the white man came but were increasingly employed as stockmen after the Territory's first cattle station was established at Springvale near Katherine in 1879. They were paid in clothes and rations. Stations frequently supported the stockmen's extended families too. Inevitably, the traditional tribal way of life disappeared for these people. The struggle for Aboriginal land rights had its origins in a strike for better wages and working conditions by 200 Gurindji stockmen at Wave Hill Station in 1966. In 1968 it became illegal to pay an Aboriginal stockman less than a white man for doing the same job.

135 mm Rokkor lens, f:5.6 1/125 sec. Kodachrome 25 ASA.

34 As the sun rises on Muckaty Station, north of Tennant Creek, a stockman is already up to check on a mare and her foal. Despite the modern convenience of four-wheel-drives, helicopters and trucks, the stockman still works six or seven days a week from dawn to dusk. Beef cattle production is the Territory's major rural industry and was its overall major industry until 1959, when it was overtaken by mining. There are 242 pastoral leases in the Northern Territory. The largest is Wave Hill Station, on the northern fringe of the Tanami Desert, which covers 12 580 square kilometres – virtually the same size as Connecticut. Abattoirs operate at Alice Springs, Tennant Creek and Katherine, and at Point Stuart and Mudginberri in the north. Live cattle are exported to Malaysia and Brunei.

28–85 mm zoom Rokkor lens, f:8 1/60 sec. Kodachrome 25 ASA.

35 An Aboriginal stockman rolls a cigarette during a smoko break on a central Australian station. Aborigines have played a part in the pastoral industry of the Northern Territory for more than 100 years. In the past, they had few other employment options. In recent years, the emergence of land rights and self-governing Aboriginal communities has removed pressures on Aboriginal boys to work for pastoral lessees. This has created some new troubles – many young Aborigines are unemployed while station managers cry out for experienced stockmen. One or two training schemes have now been set up to teach the stockman's skills to a few eager boys from Aboriginal communities.

200 mm Rokkor lens, f:5.6 1/60 sec. Kodachrome 25 ASA.

36 A Tiwi Aborigine from Bathurst Island, 80 kilometres north of Darwin, wears an intricately painted face and beard for a pukumani burial ceremony. According to Tiwi custom, one purpose of the paint is to protect the wearer from evil spirits. In Aboriginal burial ceremonies, elaborate rites are enacted not only to ensure immortality for the deceased among the great creative spirits of the Dreaming, but also to protect the living from the fury of a totemic spirit scorned by a disrespectful burial. Totems are the spirits of creatures which serve as agents between Aborigines and their deities.

135 mm Rokkor lens, direct flash at night, f:5.6 Kodachrome 64 ASA.

37 Yellow flowers (*Nymphoides* sp) cover the surface of a swamp dotted by paperbark trees in Kakadu National Park. Yellow Waters takes its name from these ephemeral flowers. Surveys have recorded 1000 species of plants in Kakadu and there are undoubtedly many more. The vast wetlands also provide a home for twenty-two species of frogs and forty-three species of fish, about a quarter of all freshwater fish species in Australia. The monarch of all these aquatic animals is the giant barramundi, which matures in freshwater streams and billabongs and swims to coastal estuaries to breed. Many fish, such as the remarkable archer fish which downs its prey with a jet of water, feed on some of the 10 000 species of insects recorded in Kakadu.

20 mm Rokkor lens, f:16 1/30 sec. Kodachrome 25 ASA.

38 A flock of pelicans flying at an even height over the glassy Magela floodplains creates a startling pattern of light and shadow. One of the best ways to find sights like this is to take an early-morning boat tour of Yellow Waters, in the Kakadu National Park. There one may see many of the 270 species of birds which live in Kakadu for all or part of the year, a third of all bird types found in Australia. About 80 species are migratory, breeding on the tundra of Siberia and other northern regions then flying to Kakadu when the Northern Hemisphere winter sets in.

Aerial – from helicopter, 28–85 mm zoom Rokkor lens, deliberate slow shutter speed 1/8 to 1/15 sec., f:8 Kodachrome 25 ASA (bracketing the shutter speed to get the desired effect).

39 Palm Valley is an enigma. Despite the searing summer heat of the desert west of Alice Springs, palms have been growing in this mostly dry tributary of the Finke River for at least 10 000 years. They are relics of a wetter and more fertile era and have survived as a result of rainwater seeping slowly through porous layers of sandstone into the gorge, where an impermeable layer of base rock prevents the water draining away. This seepage can continue through many years of drought. The palms, *Livistona mariae*, are found nowhere else in the world and grow one metre every ten years, eventually reaching thirty metres. Another plant found in the valley, the MacDonnell Range cycad, originated 200 million years ago, long before the *Livistona*.

Backlighting against dark cliff, 200 mm Rokkor lens, f:5.6 1/60 sec. Kodachrome 25 ASA.

40 Stone pillars form a colonnade leading eerily into the mysterious geological formation on the Arnhem Land plateau which has been labelled 'The Ruined City'. The formation is regarded as an intensely sacred site by tribal Aborigines and it is said that no white man has ever been further than its perimeter. Even among Aborigines, only the most knowledgeable of tribal elders are permitted to enter to perform religious rituals. Little is known about the 'city', but the pillars are probably composed of sandstone and conglomerates which have survived the erosion of surrounding sedimentary material. The formation of the Arnhem Land plateau began 2000 million years ago.

20 minutes before sunrise, 20 mm Rokkor lens, f:8 8 sec., tripod.

41 This is what the claypan in the centre of Rainbow Valley looks like for most of the year – not a skerrick of vegetation and as hard as concrete. But the inland is not all like this, for how would 400 species of plants survive if it were? Central Australian species are adept at finding and conserving moisture in an environment of unrelenting aridity. Aboriginal people survived in the desert for thousands of years by careful management of natural resources and by centring their activities around permanent waterholes.

20 mm Rokkor lens, f:16 1/30 sec. Kodachrome 25 ASA Pro.

42 Rainbow Valley lies to the south of Alice Springs in a fairly inaccessible region which may receive as little as 125 millimetres of rain in a year. It is this fact which makes the sight of water lapping at the base of the valley's rainbow-coloured cliffs so remarkable. The shallow and very temporary lake takes its cloudy colour from the substance of the flat claypan upon which it lies. Once the lake evaporates the clay becomes as hard as stone. Under the pitiless summer sun it contracts and breaks into crazy paving.

20 mm Rokkor lens, 20 minutes after sunset, tripod, f:5.6/8, bracketing to compensate for reciprocity failure. 4 sec., 8 sec., 16 sec. Correct exposure about 8 sec. Kodachrome 25 ASA.

43 A rainbow arcs over Rainbow Valley in a rare communion of namesakes. Rainfall around this central Australian landmark is infrequent and the rainbow name derives from the bright colours on the surfaces of rocky outcrops, rather than the number of rainbow sightings in the valley. The reddish colours are the result of the oxidation of iron deposits. These were embedded in sediments laid down millions of years ago beneath an inland sea. Rainbow Valley sandstone was saved from being cut into building blocks by the declaration of the area as a protected reserve.

20 mm Rokkor lens, f:8 1/60 sec. Kodachrome 25 ASA Pro. The conditions here were identical to those in photograph 5. However, this rainbow lasted for 20 minutes.

44 This husband-and-wife team are the publicans at Barrow Creek, a tiny roadside community 280 kilometres north of Alice Springs on the Stuart Highway. About a dozen people live in the hamlet, which is dominated by a petrol station, store and pub all rolled into one, and a building built as a repeater station for the overland telegraph line in the 1870s. Like many other isolated communities, Barrow Creek has an annual race meeting which draws people together from a wide radius. It is the biggest day of the year. Barrow Creek even has its own rough-and-ready golf course.

28–85 mm zoom Rokkor lens, f:8 1/60 sec. Kodachrome 64 ASA Pro.

45 You can always pick the travellers who reckon they'll be back in Barrow Creek one day – their names are written on their money at the Barrow Creek Bank. The wall of the pub started out as a place where locals could pin up a bit of spare cash, just in case they ran a bit short when they badly needed a drink. A savings bank was born the moment a name was written on the first deposit and a drawing pin connected it to the wall. Now travellers visiting the roadside pub are getting in on the act by leaving banknotes just for the fun of it. After all, there's always the possibility one might find oneself in Barrow Creek again on a hot day.

28–85 mm zoom Rokkor lens, f:5.6/8 direct flash. Kodachrome 64 ASA Pro.

46 A traditional Australian beach umbrella on a Darwin beach provides welcome protection from the damaging effects of the sun. Ultra-violet light is more intense in the tropical north than in southern parts of Australia because the sun lies more directly overhead – the UV light consequently passes through the earth's atmosphere at a more direct angle than in temperate zones and less of it is deflected. Doctors and health authorities are presently attempting to generate a wider under-standing in tropical communities of the heightened risks of skin cancer.

28–85 mm zoom Rokkor lens, f:11 1/60 sec. Kodachrome 64 ASA.

47 This girl relaxing on a Gove beach could almost be floating in a cloud, but the white foreground is part of the broad expanse of brilliant white beach which fringes the Gove Peninsula in the far north-east corner of the Top End. Other parts of the peninsula are dominated by red cliffs, noticed and reported by the navigator Matthew Flinders in 1803. They were bauxite deposits and Gove is now the site of a massive bauxite mining operation and alumina refinery. The land is leased from the Aborigines who were granted Arnhem Land by the Australian Government in the early 1970s. The town which serves the mine is called Nhulunbuy. It is populated by 4000 workers and their families and is one of the most isolated communities in Australia.

200 mm Rokkor lens, f:8 1/125 sec. Kodachrome 64 ASA.

48 The spectacular fifth canyon of the Katherine Gorges is one of thirteen ravines gouged into the Arnhem Land plateau east of Katherine. The gorges began to form during the age of the dinosaurs when storm-waters rushed into criss-cross fissures developing on the earth's surface. The annual battering of water over twenty-five million years has turned these fissures into deep gorges. In some places, the walls tower 75 metres above the Katherine River. The gorges zig-zag at right angles to one another through a grid pattern of earth faults. They are now part of a 180 000-hectare park. For thousands of years the area was home to the Djauan Aborigines and evidence of their art can be seen high up on the sides of the gorges.

20 mm Rokkor lens, f:11 1/60 sec. Kodachrome 64 ASA.

49 A desert oak near Gosse Bluff, west of Alice Springs. Those who come to central Australia expecting to see a featureless desert are invariably surprised when they find a region rich in well-adapted vegetation. There are almost 400 species of plants and trees upon the undulating red plains and the ranges. The hardy spinifex is everywhere and dotted all about are the stately desert oaks, which are actually native she-oaks. The trees grow where underground water lies close to the surface and the fine feathery leaves help to guard precious moisture against the effects of 40-degree summer heat.

28–85 mm zoom Rokkor lens, f:5.6 1/125 sec. Kodachrome 64 ASA.

50 A mural painted by students adorns a wall of the Darwin High School. It depicts a member of the Larakia Tribe, silhouetted against a blood-red tropical sunset. He stares out over beautiful Fannie Bay from the cliffs where the school now stands on Bullocky Point, one of the most scenic locations in Darwin. The Larakia Aborigines were the original inhabitants of the peninsula upon which Darwin was established in 1869. Children in Darwin have been encouraged to paint colourful murals around their schools as well as on many of the city's bus shelters and even an old pipeline running into town alongside the Stuart Highway.

28–85 mm zoom Rokkor lens, f:5.6 1/60 sec. Kodachrome 25 ASA.

51 Perhaps it's the brashness of the climate and the blueness of southern skies which encourages Australians to turn their cities into kaleidoscopes of colour. Whatever it is, visitors often voice their surprise at the things the locals take for granted, like bright blue and red roofs. In Darwin, the most vivid city of all, the colour asserts itself in various ways – in shopfronts like this takeaway store, in the blue-green sea, in the luxuriant gardens of palms, bougainvilleas and frangipanis and in the bright summer clothes worn all year round.

28–85 mm zoom Rokkor lens, f:8 1/125 sec. Kodachrome 25 ASA.

52 The Devil's Marbles are perhaps the most mystifying of all landmarks in the Northern Territory. Hundreds of large boulders, in varying states of roundness, lie scattered on both sides of the Stuart Highway in a small reserve 115 kilometres south of Tennant Creek. It is as if some prehistoric giant had flung a bag of marbles upon a little patch of the continent. To the Warumungu Aboriginal people of the region, the boulders possess a deep spiritual significance deriving from their origins in the Dreamtime. Geologists say the rocks were once part of a single granite block which split into large rectangular pieces and gradually weathered into spherical shapes.

20 mm Rokkor lens, f:8 1/60 sec. Ektachrome 64 ASA.

53 Chambers Pillar is an oddly majestic landmark which stands about 160 kilometres south of Alice Springs. It rises 34 metres above a low mound and is about 6 metres wide. Explorer John McDouall Stuart became the first white man to see Chambers Pillar in 1860 and he named it in honour of his patron, the Adelaide businessman James Chambers. Six hundred million years ago a vanishing inland sea left behind a sedimentary layer of sand and pebbles to the height of the pillar. Erosion lowered the plain to its present level but Chambers Pillar remained because it was composed of a stronger conglomerate mixture. The Aborigines know it as 'Idacowra' or 'Etikaura', which mean place of the adulterous male.

20 mm Rokkor lens. Before sunrise, f:5.6/8 4 sec.

54 Standing like a waif among the tough swamp-grasses of a Kakadu billabong, a solitary flower appears to wait for the thunderstorm threatening beyond the trees. More than 1500 millimetres of rain can fall in the north of the Top End during summer – 60 inches in the old measure. Some inland regions are lucky if they get five. This discrepancy explains the striking contrast in the flora of the Northern Territory: the luxuriant greenery of its far north and the tenacious, water-conserving scrub of the south.

20 mm Rokkor lens, f:11 1/60 sec. Ektachrome 64 ASA.

55 Islands of red earth rise out of Lake Amadeus, a mostly dry salt lake south-west of Alice Springs just north of Ayers Rock. In 1872, the explorer Ernest Giles travelled along the northern edge of Lake Amadeus and saw the Olgas, but was prevented from reaching them by the impassable nature of the lake. Oil and gas have been discovered in the sedimentary layers of the Amadeus Basin. The gas is now pumped to Darwin along a $280-million, 1500-kilometre pipeline to fuel the city's new power station. Oil from the Mereenie field in the basin is distilled at Alice Springs.

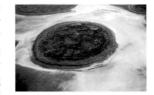

Aerial – 28–85 mm zoom Rokkor lens, f:5.6 1/125 sec. Ektachrome 64 ASA.

56 One could hardly imagine a more lonely plant than this, clinging tenaciously to the shifting red sand of a dune in the Simpson Desert. In fact, the Simpson is home to numerous species of animals and perennial plants, unlike many other famous deserts of the world. Emus, dingoes and camels roam its plains, and desert cane-grass and spinifex offer protection from the elements for smaller creatures. When it rains the desert floor becomes a beautiful carpet of ephemeral wildflowers. Seeds may lie dormant for years before rainwater soaks into the parched sand to vitalise them.

20 mm Rokkor lens, f:11 1/60 sec. Kodachrome 25 ASA.

57 Corrugations made by the wind snake across a sand dune in the Simpson Desert near the Northern Territory–Queensland border. The first explorer to enter the Simpson was Charles Sturt in 1845. The experience almost broke his heart. He was looking for a fabled inland sea, a doomed mission since there had been no such thing in Australia for 600 million years. In the desert Stuart wrote: 'This terrible, dreadful country ... The view from one of the ridges is the most terrific and cheerless man has ever gazed upon ... I shall envy the man who shall first place the flag of our native country in the centre of our adopted one.'

20 mm Rokkor lens, f:11 1/60 sec. Kodachrome 25 ASA.

58 Returning from a swim in the sea, an Aboriginal boy from Bathurst Island looks hesitantly at the photographer. The Tiwi Aborigines of Bathurst Island and neighbouring Melville Island speak their own unique language and are a gregarious people, fond of celebrations and renowned worldwide for their art. For a long time in their history they believed they were the only people on earth. Tiwi means 'we, the people'. A Catholic mission was established on Bathurst Island in 1907 and it still has considerable social influence in the community. In 1978, ownership of Bathurst Island was transferred from the Crown to the Tiwi Land Council, composed of tribal Aborigines.

200 mm Rokkor lens, f:5.6 1/60 sec. Kodachrome 25 ASA. Exposed for Aboriginal face.

59 An Aboriginal man from Yirrkala, in the far north-east corner of the Territory, sits in mourning during a burial ceremony. Mortuary rites can continue for several days, even weeks, and follow a time-honoured sequence. White clay is painted on the face and body to bring the living into communion with the spirits of their ancestors. Macassan fishermen from the Celebes visited the Yirrkala Aborigines regularly over many centuries until 1906 and some of the Islamic chants the Macassans sang as they raised their masts and sails to depart have evolved into the funeral songs of coastal Aborigines.

200 mm Rokkor lens, f:5.6 1/60 sec. Kodachrome 64 ASA.

60 As well as bringing welcome respite from intense humidity, the northern dry season soaks every last drop of moisture from large tracts of the Top End. Swamps which teemed with plant and animal life during the wet season eventually dry up and crack, becoming rock-hard. Whereas most white people living in the Top End simply separate the year climatically into the Wet and the Dry, Aborigines recognise six seasons, each determined by distinct changes in weather conditions, vegetation and animal life. The rainy season is marked at one end by the breeding of the magpie geese and at the other by the commotion of the tree crickets.

Aerial – 28–85 mm zoom Rokkor lens, f:5.6 1/125 sec. Kodachrome 25 ASA.

61 Wet-season swamps in the Top End can be deceptive. The sheer volume of densely packed vegetation can so expertly hide the water beneath that the swamp takes on the appearance of a pasture fringed by wildflowers. In some cases the stems of these water-lily wildflowers are more than two metres long. In one sense at least, the seasonal swamp lilies of the north are like the wildflowers of the parched central deserts – both come to life at an explosive rate when the rains arrive. As monsoonal storms lash the Top End, the rivers and creeks overflow their banks, re-creating the swamps over last year's cracked soils.

Aerial – 28–85 mm zoom Rokkor lens, f:5.6 1/125 sec. Ektachrome 64 ASA.

62 Pelicans swimming on the Magela floodplains at sunrise. Pelicans are often seen in pairs, hunting for fish and saltwater or freshwater crustaceans. Their nests are simply a depression in the earth which they progressively ply with grasses and sticks as the two or three eggs incubate. They are found throughout Australia in both salty river estuaries and freshwater inland lakes. In Kakadu, these adaptable birds share the waterways with the more specialised species which live only in the tropical north – birds such as the burdekin duck, green pygmy goose, pied heron, magpie goose and jabiru.

Aerial – captured in the last sunlight. 135 mm Rokkor lens, f:2.8 1/60 sec. Ektachrome 64 ASA.

63 This plumed egret on Yellow Waters in Kakadu National Park appears to be drying its feathers, but it is just as likely to be catching fish in a most ingenious manner. By extending its wings while standing motionless in shallow water, the egret creates a shady area which attracts aquatic animals. These animals believe the shade has been provided by a piece of vegetation or overhanging branch, a belief which invariably leads to their demise. Despite being listed as nomadic and rather rare in Australia, plumed egrets are quite easily spotted on Yellow Waters.

600 mm APO Rokkor lens, f:8 1/125 sec. Kodachrome 25 ASA. Tripod mounted in boat.

64 Lotus birds, up bright and early on Yellow Waters in Kakadu National Park, wait for something to happen in the way of aquatic food. The lotus bird is a marvellous creature, for it walks on water. This remarkable achievement has earned it the nickname of the 'Christ bird'. One of its other nicknames, 'lily trotter', gives it away. It spends its whole life walking, feeding and breeding upon lily pads or indeed any scrap of vegetation floating on the surface of swamps and lagoons, a feat made possible by its enormously long toes. It has a distinctive comb which ranges in colour from yellow to deep red, depending on the bird's emotional state.

600 mm APO Rokkor lens, f:6.3 1/60 sec. Kodachrome 25 ASA, tripod.

65 Surrounded by clumps of paperbark trees, geese and ducks stand and swim in groups upon Yellow Waters in Kakadu National Park. When the wet season runs itself dry and the circumferences of the swamps creep ever inward, large billabongs such as Yellow Waters remain to sustain life until the rains return. For many months they are magnets drawing in a diverse range of creatures, and the dry season is an excellent time to see many of Kakadu's 270 species of birds concentrated in one place. Even so, one would still have to venture into the rocky outcrops of the escarpment country to see a bird like the chestnut-quilled rock pigeon, or into the woodlands to find the great bowerbird.

200 mm Rokkor lens, f:5.6/8 1/125 sec. Ektachrome 64 ASA.

66 The construction of the Diamond Beach Hotel-Casino in Darwin in the early 1980s ushered in a new era of sophistication for the former frontier town. The days of limited choice were over. Two five-star international hotels have since been established in Darwin. Built at a cost of $30 million in an adventurous modern style, the casino stands beside Mindil Beach under the rising slopes of the Botanic Gardens. It was extensively refurbished in 1986. The casino has proved a Mecca not only for visitors but for the people of Darwin and its main gaming room is never far from full.

35 mm Rokkor lens, after sunset, f:5.6 8 sec., tripod. Kodachrome 25 ASA. Image was then flipped to create mirror-image for use in advertising.

67 A girl lazes on an airbed in the pool of the Sheraton Hotel at the Yulara Resort. Yulara was built near Ayers Rock in 1984 at a cost of $160 million. The sail-like shades which are a special feature of the resort are part of a unique overall design which won the complex a major Australian architectural award. The desert-bound resort includes two hotels, holiday cabins, a camping ground, a visitors' centre, staff accommodation, a school, a community hall and various shops. It is 16 kilometres from Ayers Rock, outside the Uluru National Park. The untidy tourist village which previously stood at the base of the monolith was demolished.

20 mm Rokkor lens, f:8/11 1/60 sec. To create a flat surface in the pool, the pump had to be turned off beforehand.

68 A boy plays with a couple of cardboard cups beside the racetrack at Timber Creek on the big day of the year – race day. With his over-sized stockman's hat and his boots, jeans and checked shirt he probably mirrors his father's appearance at half the size. Timber Creek lies on the Victoria River and on the road from Katherine to the Western Australian border. It has a population of about thirty but on race day the number swells to 1500 or more. The big event is the Timber Creek Cup, run over 1600 metres for a cash prize of $3500. The leader out of the barrier always has a big advantage – the others can't see for dust.

200 mm Rokkor lens, f:5.6 1/125 sec. Kodachrome 25 ASA.

69 From his bottle-crate perch on the verandah of the Barrow Creek Hotel, a young boy keeps an eye on events along the Stuart Highway, the transportation backbone of the Territory. The Barrow Creek settlement evolved after a repeater station was built there for the overland telegraph line in 1872. In 1874, the stationmaster, J. L. Stapleton, and John Franks were killed by hostile warriors of the Kaititja tribe. The Kaititja and their northern neighbours, the Warramunga, bitterly resented European intrusion in the 19th century. A punitive expedition was organised from Adelaide and, according to the official report, eleven Aborigines were shot in the bush. Most other sources put the real figure at more than fifty.

28–85 mm zoom Rokkor lens, f:5.6 1/60 sec. Kodachrome 25 ASA.

70 Wild camels like this group on Allambi Station, south-east of Alice Springs, are now a permanent feature of desert areas. In fact, Australia has the largest population of wild camels in the world. They are the descendants of animals brought to Australia more than 100 years ago to help open up the arid interior of the continent. They performed admirably, their great advantages over horses and bullocks being that they could last as long as two months in the desert without water, needed no shoes and could cross sandy terrain while living off the land. These present-day animals are so healthy that some of them are being exported back to their countries of origin to rejuvenate diseased dromedary stock.

Aerial – 28–85 mm zoom Rokkor lens, f:8 1/60 sec. Kodachrome 64 ASA.

71 The large numbers of wild horses in the Northern Territory are a legacy of the 1914–18 war, when pastoralists in cental Australia bred mounts for the Indian army. After the war ended, the remaining horses were released into the wild. They thrived in inaccessible regions and soon began to multiply in all parts of the Territory. No one is certain how many there are but most agree that a population of one million is not inconceivable. In arid regions, wild horses threaten the pastoral industry by knocking down fences and competing with cattle for feed. As a result, many have been shot from helicopters in an attempt to keep numbers down. An abattoir in Tennant Creek exports horsemeat to Japan and Europe.

Aerial – deliberate selection of slow shutter speeds. Low-flying helicopter moving approximately same speed as horses. 28–85 mm zoom Rokkor lens, f:16 approx. 1/8 sec. but bracketing the shutter speed for the right effect. Kodachrome 25 ASA Pro.

72 This windmill and these watertanks silhouetted against the evening sky at Barrow Creek are reminders of the essential element which holds sway over the life of the inland, or anywhere for that matter. Without reasonable quantities of accessible water, many regions of the Northern Territory would never have been settled by humans – black or white. Despite its arid surface, much of the inland lies above underground water. The Great Artesian Basin of western Queensland extends into the south-east part of the territory and meets other basins which extend west and north-west. Windmills pump the water from these basins into great storage tanks which are built on stands to provide water pressure at ground-level.

28–85 mm zoom Rokkor lens, f:8 1/60 sec. Kodachrome 64 ASA Pro.

73 An incandescent rainbow-like sunset silhouettes the wiry trees of central Australia. These beautiful twilights are more subtle than the extravagant tropical sunsets of the Top End. Desert light – which is not hazy at all – has a mother-of-pearl quality. It was this clarity and a high percentage of cloud-free days which led the American *Sky and Telescope* magazine to name central Australia as the best place in the world to see Halley's Comet in 1985–86. The night sky is so bright with stars, one can read a newspaper by its light.

20 mm Rokkor lens, f:5.6/8 1 sec., tripod. Kodachrome 25 ASA.

74 The surface of a claypan dries, hardens and contracts into scaly patterns as the dry season wears on. Not all the wetlands and waterholes disappear during the Dry, and those which remain sustain animal life until the rain cycle begins again. The plants of the north take their chances, dying in the dry season but leaving the seeds which will turn the landscape green within days of the first rainstorms.

20 mm Rokkor lens, f:11 1/125. Kodachrome 64 ASA.

75 The sky splashes traces of blue across a reflection in a rock pool at the base of King's Canyon, a breathtaking gorge in the George Gill Ranges, west of Alice Springs. A permanent spring and the seepage of water into the ravine maintains a garden of 600 species of plants, many of them rare. One of these plants, the skeleton fork fern, is a living relic of an era 300 million years ago. Entry into the garden is not easy – visitors must either descend through a crevice and a narrow cave, or cross a rock ledge and climb down a cliff face.

135 mm Rokkor lens, f:5.6/8 1/60 sec. Ektachrome 64 ASA.

76 Aboriginal ceremonies are held for a variety of reasons but all have the unifying feature of communion with the spirits of ancestors living in the non-physical world of the Dreaming. In central Australian ceremonies such as this, leaves tied into anklets make a rustling noise to add to the music created by didgeridoos, knocking boomerangs, singing and the mimicking of animal calls by the dancers. Animal totemism is also evident in the feather headdresses and body decorations. Most Aboriginal dance movements are made at the shoulder, hip and knee joints while the torso is held still in a semi-crouching position.

28–85 mm zoom Rokkor lens, f:5.6 1/15 sec. Ektachrome 64 ASA. A mixture of tungsten and daylight.

77 Tiwi Aboriginal children are always to be found playing in the surf on the shores of Bathurst Island north of Darwin. The Tiwi people are renowned for their exuberance and friendliness but in the early years of European colonisation they were among the most fierce of all Australian tribes. The Tiwi are the descendants of the second wave of prehistoric Aboriginal travellers to come to Australia during the Ice Age. After a long period of hostility the Tiwi people eventually made their peace with the white man and resigned themselves to a new era. Today they preserve their traditions while they make money the white man's way – by exporting art to Australian capital cities, Europe and the United States.

200 mm Rokkor lens, f:5.6/8 1/125 sec. Kodachrome 64 ASA.

78 A rare and beautiful sight: Ayers Rock in a blue mood as streaks of rainwater send silver ribbons from summit to sand. A meagre 125 millimetres of rain may fall on the Rock in a year, if it falls at all, and when it does, strange things happen. In the myriad pools on top of the Rock, green shield shrimps called Apus spring to life after lying for months or years as eggs amongst the dust. Despite existing as a species for 150 million years, the life of one of these small creatures is over almost as soon as it has begun. It rapidly matures, mates and lays its eggs before evaporation steals its life away. Once again the eggs wait, for years perhaps, until the next rains.

I arrived at Ayers Rock after sunset and it was pouring with rain. Camera was rested on the open window of the car and I pushed Ektachrome 64 ASA to 250 ASA to give me an acceptable shutter speed. f:5.6 1 sec. 28 mm Rokkor lens.

79 More than just a famous landmark, Ayers Rock is the definitive symbol of the Australian centre. It seems to hold a peculiar fascination for all Australians and most feel the urge to visit it sooner or later. City-born Aborigines join the exodus to the heartland to gaze on the object which held their ancestors in thrall for many thousands of years. Those who climb the Rock find today's standard 1600-metre ascent rather easier than William Gosse found his path up a steep ridge in 1873. No one will ever know if the Aborigines climbed the Rock before Gosse, who was the first white man to the top. Their religion may well have discouraged them.

200 mm Rokkor lens, f:5.6 1/125 sec. Kodachrome 25 ASA.

80 A finder's hands cradle a 100 g gold nugget from the Kurrinilly Mine, 230 kilometres south-east of Tennant Creek. They belong to Ray Hall who, with wife Maria, discovered a major gold-bearing reef five metres underground in November 1987. It was this nugget which convinced Ray Hall that the reef was there, despite the fact that the mine was first pegged during the heady goldrush days of Tennant Creek in the 1930s. The Halls' find made big news around the country and there was talk that the reef was worth millions. Now the estimates are more conservative but nevertheless the mine is an excellent prospect. A mining company has negotiated with the Halls to operate the claim and will extract and crush the ore.

50 mm macro Rokkor lens, f:8/11 1/60 sec. Kodachrome 64 ASA Pro.

81 Ray and Maria Hall made their dreams come true when they struck it rich after years of fruitless gold prospecting in hot, dusty and fly-ridden conditions. The rainbow which appeared when they were photographed at their diggings south of Tennant Creek provided a fitting symbol to their very real pot of gold. Ray and Maria spend each winter prospecting in the Territory and the summer on their farm in Victoria. They first came to Tennant Creek in 1981, when Ray arrived for a six-month stint at the local meatworks. A shoulder injury a few years later ended Ray's meatworks career and he and Maria decided to turn their prospecting hobby into a full-time occupation. In a way Ray was simply following a family tradition. Both his grandfather and uncle had been prospectors.

28–85 mm zoom Rokkor lens, f:8 1/125 sec. Kodachrome 64 ASA Pro.

82 The breaking of a new day reveals another aspect of Yellow Waters as early morning mist drifts amongst wetland trees in Kakadu National Park. Yellow Waters is one of the most accessible regions of the park, and one of the most diverse, but it is only part of the whole spectacular story. Kakadu contains examples of all three major types of terrain in Arnhem Land – the sandstone plateau, the undulating country west of the escarpment and the lowlands of lagoons and billabongs. The park takes its name from the Gagadju Aboriginal people who have lived in the region for millennia.

28–85 mm zoom Rokkor lens, f:8 1 sec. Kodachrome 25 ASA.

83 The darter prefers to be alone and is often found in secluded wetland areas. Seen here in the first light at Yellow Waters in Kakadu, the darter is the only Australian representative of the family called *Anhingidae*. A large bird, it resembles a cormorant, although it has a much longer neck. The darter takes its name from the action of its neck while hunting fish underwater. Swimming beneath the surface of rivers and swamps, it keeps its neck bent until it gets close enough to a fish to suddenly straighten up and spear its prey.

200 mm Rokkor lens, early morning, f:5.6 1/60 sec. Kodachrome 25 ASA Pro.

84 A multitude of separate ethnic groups make up Darwin's population, the most recognisably multicultural in Australia. Nowhere is the mixture more evident than in the schools, where children from vastly different cultures learn and play together. Parap Primary School has counted almost fifty different nationalities among its pupils. Here, Parap students stand before a mural at the local shopping centre.

28–85 mm zoom Rokkor lens, f:8 1/60 sec. Kodachrome 25 ASA Pro. This photo was fun to take – great children.

85 This mural at the Darwin High School was painted by students and, as a representation of their 1980s environment, it provides a contemporary parallel to the ancient Aboriginal rock art of the Top End. Its bright primary colours reflect both the modernity and vitality of Darwin. The site of the school on Bullocky Point has itself a colourful past. In 1917, the huge international Vestey's corporation established a meatworks on the Point. It employed 500 men and covered ten acres but lasted just three years before it was closed in 1920, owing to shipping difficulties and union problems. As it was the major source of employment in Darwin, the meatworks' closure hit the city hard and many people left.

28–85 mm zoom Rokkor lens, f:5.6 1/60 sec. Kodachrome 25 ASA Pro.

86 On a typically clear night, the distinctive sails of the Sheraton Hotel are silhouetted against the sky above the Yulara Tourist Resort, 16 kilometres from Ayers Rock. The sails form part of Yulara's unique character and were designed to reflect the sun's fierce inland glare. When the air is still they seem to lure a faint breeze from nowhere. Built at a cost of $160 million and officially opened in November 1984, Yulara aims to cater for every pocket and it has its own resident population. The children of the staff attend a village school. Yulara is a remarkable community: a man-made island in a sea of sand. It is also unobtrusive and almost invisible from the top of Ayers Rock.

20 mm Rokkor lens, f:5.6 2 sec. and bracketing. Reflection is created by the swimming pool with the pump turned off. Moon has been added later to create a more realistic night view. Kodachrome 25 ASA.

87 Aussat satellite dishes, installed in 1985, point into space beyond a pink sunset at Palmerston, one of Darwin's most recently developed residential areas. The Aussat satellite communication system transmits video, text, data and voice channels. Its biggest Darwin customers are the Australian Broadcasting Corporation, Telecom and companies drilling for oil from rigs in the Timor Sea. It's a far cry from the single strand of wire which linked Australia to England in 1872 and was itself a great technological achievement.

200 mm Rokkor lens, f:4 1/60 sec. Kodachrome 25 ASA Pro.

88 Shaking the water from its only partially webbed feet, a magpie goose beats skyward in Kakadu National Park. Magpie geese live in their thousands on the Top End wetlands and the sound of myriad beating wings is deafening when a startled flock takes to the air. They have an unusual breeding arrangement in which one male mates with two females. Both mothers lay their eggs in the same nest and all three adults spend several months together incubating, feeding and training the offspring. In 1974, the bigamous magpie goose was chosen as the symbol for the first International Bird Congress held in Australia.

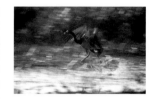

After two early mornings and many rolls of film I got this shot of a magpie goose taking off. 500 mm Rokkor lens, f:8 1/15 sec. Tripod and panning with the bird. Ektachrome 64 ASA.

89 Each year when the wet season arrives, huge populations of magpie geese spread out over the floodplains of the Top End to breed. They are the most abundant birds in the north and are often seen in their thousands, as this scene on the Adelaide River floodplain shows. Almost 400 000 of them were counted in the Top End in 1980. Half that number were found on one South Alligator River swamp alone, vast though it was. Magpie geese once lived throughout south-eastern Australia but hunting and the destruction of their habitat by white settlers drove populations to the safer wetlands of the north.

Aerial – 28–85 mm zoom Rokkor lens, f:5.6 1/125 sec. Ektachrome 64 ASA Pro.

90 As early-morning sunlight captures the dust in his wake, a trainer gallops a racehorse along the dry bed of the Todd River in Alice Springs. Central Australians are fond of horseracing and one of the highlights of their year is the Alice Springs Cup in May. People come from hundreds of kilometres around for the carnival get-together and owners bring their horses from all over Australia. As for the Todd River, it rarely has water in it. When it does it can overflow its banks within an hour.

28–85 mm zoom Rokkor lens, f:5.6 1/125 sec. Kodachrome 64 ASA. This photo was shot for the book *The Racing Game*.

91 A jockey's beautifully polished boots and dazzling breeches strike a discordant note in a city renowned for its casualness. This photograph was taken at the Darwin Turf Club. The highlights of the racing year in the Top End are the St Patrick's Day Cup in March and the Darwin Cup in August, which attract entries from interstate. Some of Darwin's most colourful stories hark back to the days of independent betting shops and the characters who ran them. The Territory's Racing and Gaming Commission put an end to all that in 1985 when it replaced the betting shops with the TAB system.

28–85 mm zoom Rokkor lens, f:5.6/8 1/60 sec. Kodachrome 64 ASA.

92 At the Mindil Beach weekend market in Darwin one may enjoy the sights and tastes of Asian cuisine cooked on the spot and some of the Territory's tropical fruits in a fresh fruit salad. There are several such cosmopolitan markets around the city. Darwin's population of more than 76 000 people is composed of almost fifty different ethnic groups and nationalities. At one time in the mid-1980s both Darwin and neighbouring Palmerston had Chinese mayors. The city's multiculturalism goes back to the last century when Chinese men came from Singapore, Hong Kong and the Kwantung province to work on the Pine Creek goldfields. For a long time the Chinese outnumbered the whites in the Top End by four to one.

28–85 mm zoom Rokkor lens, f:5.6 1/60 sec. Kodachrome 64 ASA.

93 Chebasio Gima is a leading pearl diver with the Darwin-based Paspaley Pearling Company, one of the world's biggest cultured-pearl producers. He works at Port Essington on the Cobourg Peninsula north-east of Darwin, where Paspaley's have a cultured-pearl farm, and at Broome in Western Australia. Chebasio Gima was recruited from the Kuni tribe of New Guinea to work in the Northern Territory's pearling industry. Since 1884, Japanese, Malays, Filipinos and Indonesians have all dived for Darwin-based companies. The Territory's healthy pearl-shell industry was dealt a mortal blow with the advent of plastic in the late 1950s but the Paspaley company has created a new industry out of the old.

28–85 mm zoom Rokkor lens, f:8 1/60 sec. Kodachrome 25 ASA Pro.

94 It is a cruel fact that despite the enticing relief it offers from the summer heat, the sea surrounding Darwin cannot be swum in for half the year. Deadly box jellyfish lurk in the shallow waters of the Top End during the wet season and there have been dozens of fatalities over the years in Darwin and settlements on the northern coast. Water sports, like the paragliding seen here off Mindil Beach, are restricted to the dry season. The famous sand bar off Myilly Point, within sight of the Diamond Beach Casino, is a popular meeting spot at low tide. On weekends, groups head out to the sand bar by boat for a picnic before the tide returns and covers it once more.

Aerial – from helicopter. 28–85 mm zoom Rokkor lens, f:5.6 1/250 sec. Kodachrome 64 ASA.

95 The Arafura Sea is shallow and cloudy all the way from the Northern Territory to the shores of New Guinea. This lack of depth contributes to its opaque green colour. The sea is strewn with reefs and it rises and falls with dramatic exaggeration upon the long flat beaches of the Territory coast. At certain moments during the Ice Age the Arafura Sea did not exist at all, since the world's oceans had fallen an incredible 150 metres. The ancestors of Australia's Aborigines walked across the resulting land bridge between New Guinea and Australia and it is likely that they once inhabited areas now covered by sea.

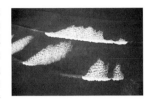

Aerial – 28–85 mm zoom Rokkor lens, f:5.6 1/250 sec. Kodachrome 64 ASA.

96 Aboriginal corroborees, like this one in central Australia, are ceremonies of singing and dancing and involve every member of the clan. As is usual with any oral tradition, learning begins at an early age. Children are encouraged to join in the dancing with their parents, although formal instruction in the functions of ritual songs and dances does not begin for boys until they have reached the age of initiation. As a young man passes through the recognised stages of maturity, he learns more of the tribal lore underlying the dances and comes to understand his responsibilities as the custodian of particular movements. The man on the left is blowing a didgeridoo, a hollow wooden pipe which emits a doleful droning sound. It is not easily mastered.

28–85 mm zoom Rokkor lens, straight flash at night, f:5.6 Ektachrome 64 ASA pushed to 125 ASA (one stop).

97 Darwin's German community celebrates St Martin's Day on 11 November each year with a lantern festival at the water gardens in Rapid Creek. According to a time-honoured tradition, children place candles inside lanterns they have made themselves and walk hand-in-hand singing German folk songs. Saint Martin was a soldier of the 4th century who is said to have cut his cloak in two in order to give half to a beggar on a winter's night. Later he became bishop of Tours in France. Many of the ethnic groups and nationalities living in Darwin retain their traditions by holding similar celebrations or by meeting in clubs and associations.

Minolta CLE Rangefinder camera, 28 mm Rokkor lens, f:5.6, one sec. Ektachrome Pro rated at 1600 ASA.

98 The city of Darwin was destined to exist – it must have been to have survived neglect, wartime bombing and two devastating cyclones in 1897 and 1974. It has become a thriving administrative and commercial centre. The first European settlement was established on the present site in 1869 and was called Palmerston. Later the name was changed to Darwin but in the early 1980s the original name was given to a new residential area 19 kilometres south of the main city. The population of this satellite city has been growing at an astonishing rate – in 1987 it was 16.7 per cent. Darwin is now an especially attractive city, well supplied with infrastructure for its industry and facilities for its people.

200 mm Rokkor lens, f:5.6 1 sec. Kodachrome 25 ASA Pro.

99 Thirty-seven Timorese refugees stand on the shores of the Timor Sea, the stretch of ocean they traversed to escape domination by Indonesia. Darwin now has a substantial and well-integrated Timorese community which has contributed much to the city's commercial life and to its multicultural vitality. Timor, 600 kilometres north-west of Darwin, is one of Australia's closest neighbours. It is hardly surprising that there are strong bonds between the two countries – Timor is not even half as far from Darwin as Alice Springs. The first people to come to Australia sailed from islands such as Timor to the Territory about 40 000 years ago.

28–85 mm zoom Rokkor lens, f:5.6/8 1/60 sec. Kodachrome 25 ASA Pro.

100 Buffaloes on the Magela floodplains in Kakadu National Park. Since their introduction to northern Australia 160 years ago, buffaloes have multiplied in the wild at an alarming rate, wreaking havoc on wetland areas. They have disturbed the delicate natural balance of Kakadu and other wetland areas by reducing waterholes and billabongs to muddy pools, devouring large quantities of aquatic plant life and breaking the banks of freshwater lagoons, allowing seawater in to kill plants and animals. The Territory Government wants to eliminate feral buffaloes from the Top End by 1992. The animals are now being shot or rounded up for the abattoir or domestication programmes.

Aerial – 28–85 mm zoom Rokkor lens, f:5.6 1/125 sec. Ektachrome 64 ASA Pro.

101 Perfectly camouflaged, a saltwater crocodile lurks among the mangroves and mud of a coastal creek in the Top End. Australian crocodiles are so well adapted to their environment that they have lived unchanged for more than 100 million years. They are the last survivors of the age of the dinosaurs. The saltwater variety, the fearful man-eaters of legend, are found in estuaries, rivers and even dry-season billabongs. They can grow to more than seven metres in length and one tonne in weight. Their numbers are now on the rise again after decades of hunting for their skins by white shooters. Their present numbers are estimated at 50 000. About 140 000 were shot between 1945 and 1972 when they were declared a protected species.

135 mm Rokkor lens, f:8 1/60 sec. Ektachrome 64 ASA.

102 A water dragon keeps a wary look-out beside a small watercourse in the Top End. If threatened, water dragons will dive into the nearest stream or pool and may remain submerged at the bottom for a considerable length of time. Another ploy is to float upside down like a piece of driftwood. They are good swimmers, pressing their legs against their bodies and using their feet and tails for propulsion. They live around creeks which are usually dry for much of the year. They are good tree climbers and runners. Adults can grow to almost a metre in length.

50 mm macro Rokkor lens, f:8 1/15 sec. Kodachrome 64 ASA.

103 The rare Oenpelli python was the first major species of python discovered in 100 years and was identified in 1977 by the Northern Territory's resident snake expert, Graeme Gow. Gow's interest was aroused when he spotted a heavy snake track leading from the Arnhem Land escarpment to a waterhole at Oenpelli. The track was bigger than any made by familiar Territory snakes and Gow reasoned it was either a freak or something new to science. After two weeks he hunted it down. When he found a second specimen a year later he was able to announce his discovery to the world. Gow believes Arnhem Land Aborigines saw the Oenpelli python as the living embodiment of their mythic Rainbow Serpent.

28–85 mm zoom Rokkor lens, f:8/11 1/60 sec. Kodachrome 25 ASA (my most patient model).

104 Just east of Kakadu, Aboriginal boys from Oenpelli play a daring game as they climb into the slippery path of a wet season waterfall on the Arnhem Land escarpment. The escarpment runs for more than 600 kilometres south of Oenpelli and is 450 metres high in parts. In Kakadu, the caves and overhanging ledges along the escarpment's base have provided a gallery for the art of Aborigines for more than 30 000 years. Kakadu is principally owned by the Gagadju people, who leased it to the Australian National Parks and Wildlife Service in 1978 for 99 years.

28–85 mm zoom Rokkor lens, f:8 1/125 sec. Kodachrome 64 ASA. I had to swim a long way to get this angle – with my camera in one hand.

105 Two Gunwinggu boys enjoying the clear waters of a pool created by rainwater draining off the Arnhem Land escarpment near Oenpelli, 300 kilometres east of Darwin. It is the local children's favourite spot and school classes go there sometimes to cool off when the weather is unbearably oppressive. Oenpelli also has a beautiful perennial billabong, but one advantage of swimming in the rock pool is that there is no chance of meeting a man-eating crocodile.

28–85 mm zoom Rokkor lens, f:11 1/30 sec. Kodachrome 64 ASA.

106 A hot-air balloon, as tall as an eight-storey building, floats serenely over the central Australian landscape. Michael Sanby established the balloon tour business in Alice Springs in the early 1980s and has since taken hundreds of parties over the region's most eye-catching scenery. The balloon's direction is dictated by the wind but the pilot maintains two-way radio contact with a support vehicle on the ground. When the balloon gets too close to the ground or a mountain range, propane gas is fired up to provide the necessary lift. The balloon floats at a height of 150 metres and travels at about 24 kilometres an hour.

Aerial – 16 mm super wide-angle Rokkor lens, f:8 1/125 sec. Kodachrome 25 ASA. Photo was taken from another balloon.

107 Racehorses and riders blend peacefully into the landscape as they round a turn on the red Alice Springs racetrack. Down beside the railings it is usually anything but peaceful as Alice Springs socialites and stock-booted stationhands shout with excitement. Territorians are renowned gamblers and horseracing is a popular sport. Every remote region has its annual race day which is invariably the highlight of the social calendar for the local community. Out in the spinifex country, the jockeys in their silks provide a colourful contrast to the dusty horsemen from the cattle stations.

Aerial – 28–85 mm zoom Rokkor lens, f:5.6 1/250 sec. Kodachrome 64 ASA. This photo was shot for the book *The Racing Game*.

108 These strange-looking structures are the living quarters of millions of termites. Inside each pillar are labyrinths of passages and ventilation shafts, armies of tireless builders and a single queen producing thousands of offspring every day. Termite mounds of various shapes and descriptions are found in many northern areas of the Territory. The tallest has been recorded at 6.7 metres. The termites use saliva and soil as building materials and are voracious eaters, as the early European settlers discovered to their chagrin and dismay. Wooden buildings and fences disintegrated within months in many cases.

Aerial – 135 mm zoom Rokkor lens, f:2.8 1/125 sec. Kodachrome 64 ASA.

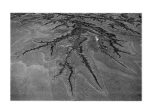

109 The tides in the Top End are some of the most powerful and extreme in the world, rising and falling by about eight metres over broad coastal flats and mangrove banks. When the tide retreats, dragging the sea backward for hundreds of metres, remarkable dendritic drainage patterns are left behind. Dendrites are tree-branch markings found on certain stones and minerals. The tidal flats occur because the sea to the north of the Top End is shallow and reef-laden. The continental shelf extends all the way to New Guinea beneath the Arafura Sea.

Aerial – 28–85 mm zoom Rokkor lens, f:5.6 1/125 sec. Kodachrome 64 ASA.

Notes for the
Amateur Photographer

I started taking photographs as a hobby in 1973 when I first arrived in Australia from Germany and was working with a large mining company. Since I travelled a good deal in my job I began to enthusiastically photograph the places I visited. During the following few years my visual perception evolved and became more refined as I gradually became aware of the subtle play between light and composition. I also began to understand the capabilities and limitations of film and camera in capturing what I was seeing. In 1976, I took the plunge and became a full-time freelance photographer. This book represents the outcome of the lessons learned in the 10-year period since that step.

I believe you have to be both aggressive and adventurous in photography. You must experiment and break the rules. If it does not work, you've learned something, but if it succeeds, you're likely to have produced a great image.

According to the rules, you should not shoot directly into the sun. However, in the presence of the diffusing effects of dust or smoke, shooting directly into the sun can produce some remarkable images (see page 68). My photograph featured on the cover of *Time* magazine in 1983 was taken during the great drought of that year, and utilised the diffusing effects of a dust storm.

When the sun has set, don't be too hasty to pack away your camera. In the afterglow of a sunset, there is a precise moment, perhaps 20 minutes following sunset, when the light exposure readings from all directions are absolutely equal. I discovered this during one of many photographic excursions to what is perhaps my favourite location, Rainbow Valley, south-east of Alice Springs. At such an instant, it is possible to capture the beautiful nuances displayed in the photograph on page 76.

The imaginative use of special effects such as producing a reflection (see page 100), or placing a moon in the night sky (see page 120), can enhance the visual impact of an image beyond that which is actually present, but which is nevertheless conceivable.

On occasion I like to convey the impression of movement – a blend of movie and still photography – as demonstrated in the aerial photograph of the stampeding brumbies on page 105. Simple tricks, such as the use of a white T-shirt as a fill-in reflector or a darkened doorway to create a dramatic black backdrop for a portrait (see page 78), all produce memorable images. Joyce Childress said to me once, "Looking at your photographs, I can actually feel the dust between my teeth."

Keep your equipment simple and know its capabilities and limitations. Don't become distracted from your subject by concerning yourself with a multitude of gadgets. I mostly work with two Minolta X-700/motor-driven camera bodies, the Rokkor 200 mm, f:2.8, 28–85 mm f:3.5 zoom, 135 mm, f:2.8 and the 20 mm f:2.8 lenses. With this basic equipment, I can handle almost any situation. I don't use colour filters during location shots – only a polarising filter when required. For special effects work I sometimes use colour correction filters. Equipment: 3 x 700 Minoltas with motor drive; Rokkor lenses from 16 mm to 800 mm; Minolta Spotmeter M; Minolta Flashmeter 3; Minolta 9000 AF with lenses; Minolta CLE and XM; Minolta XE-1.

We all have our mentors and mine has always been the New York photographer Pete Turner. Long before meeting him I'd admired the brilliant use of bright, bold primary colours in his extraordinary photographs. Working with him I observed his approach of studying a specific subject for hours on end, seeking the correct angle and light in order to capture the ultimate image. He taught me to think and concentrate, not just to shoot roll after roll of film of everything around me. I'd like to thank him for sharing his knowledge and friendship with me.

An essential ingredient for me to a successful career in photography is travel. To be immersed in new and different cultures continues to stimulate my imagination. Pete Turner was once asked what it is that drives him to continue to produce new and exciting images year after year. He replied, "Tickets, tickets, tickets!"

Gunther Deichmann

In 1986 Gunther Deichmann was named by the *Bulletin* as one of the leading professional photographers in the country. He is a freelance photographer based in Darwin and his work ranges from photojournalism to advertising to special effects.

BOOKS
Time-Life, Reader's Digest, BBC (London)

Gunther Deichmann has completed the photography for seven books including *Australia's Natural Wonders* and has contributed to countless others.

MAGAZINES
National Geographic, Signature, Der Spiegel (Germany), PM (Germany), New Look (France), Penthouse, Geo (Germany), Sawasdee (Thai International), Audubon (USA), Airone (Italy), Minolta Mirror (Japan), Merian (Germany), major work with Stern (Germany), cover of Time.

Bunte (Germany), National Magazine (Africa), Hobby Magazine (Germany), Schweizer Illustrierte (Switzerland), Zeit Magazine (Germany), BBC London (UK), CBS/Sony (Japan — record jacket 'Cusco Planet Voyage'), Terre Sauvage (France), New York Times (USA), Sud Deutsche Zeitung (Germany), Playboy (Australia).

CLIENTS
Royal Brunei Airlines, Sheraton Hotels, Department of Tourism (DOT) Philippines, Philippines Convention and Visitors Corporation (PCVC), Photokina (Agfa/Minolta) Philippines.

AWARDS
1985
Australian Professional Landscape Photographer of the Year.

1986
A collection of Gunther Deichmann's photographs in an Australian tourist booklet won for its publishers a unique clean sweep of prizes in its category at the International Travel Awards — first prize for Best Domestic Brochure, first prize for Best International Brochure and the National Tourism Award.

An advertising campaign using one of Gunther Deichmann's photographs won awards at the Art Directors Club Awards in Melbourne.

A photo-essay for Thai International won him a PATA Category award and he has been on the PATA Gold Awards Honour Roll in Osaka, Japan, since 1987.

1987
The NT Press Club Annual Media Awards 'Pictorial Excellence Award'. The 'Sheraton Award' for a pictorial promotion of tourism in NT.

Gunther Deichmann has won an impressive 12 merit awards from the Australian Institute of Professional Photography since 1982.

He is featured in a documentary called *Visions in the Making,* which has been screened on the ABC.

Gunther Deichmann's work is now taking him increasingly to Asia. In the past he has worked in some of the most remote parts of Australia as well as places such as Tahiti, Norfolk Island, Nauru Island and Pitcairn Island.

Acknowledgements

Gunther Deichmann would like to thank the following for their assistance and support over the years:

Kathy Deichmann, Misha, Sasha and Heidi; Irene Deichmann; Bernd Deichmann; Gary and Marlene Wood; Kevin Hamdorf; Ian Marshall; Ray Grimshaw (Ernst and Whinney); Dr Ean Ong; Ray Scanlon (Arts Council of NT); Dr Colin Jack-Hinton (NT Art Gallery and Museum); Bob Young; Eric Poole (NT Tourist Commission); John Boutcher and staff; Adrian Schoots; John Everingham (Bangkok); Tim Cope; Melanie Z. Siena (Manila); George Gittoes (Sydney).

Pete Turner (New York); Steve Krongard (New York); Lee McElfresh and Betty Greenhatch (Melbourne); Rob and Lynn Slatyer (Melbourne); Guy Lamonthe (Melbourne); Robert Hoebel (Germany); John-Paul Ferrero and Ester Beaton (Sydney); Wayne Miles; David Haigh; Peg Rushton (Kodak, Melbourne); Lyndon Michelson; Joyce Childress (Sydney).

Sheraton Hotels of the NT; Chebasio Gima; children and staff of Parap Primary School; Gil and Ludi and the Darwin Timorese community; Adrian Bartlett (Lasercolour, Adelaide); Rolf Schultz (Chromocolour, Adelaide); Karl Timms (Rotor Services, Darwin); TNT (Darwin); Bill King, Chris Felstedt and staff (Destination Australia); Max Whitehead (Centralian, Melbourne); Larry Anderson (Darwin); Denise Kitchen (Territory Editorial); Steve Bunk; Max and Phyllis Davidson; Aboriginal communities of Arnhem Land, Bathurst Island, Roper River and Central Australia; Noel Fullerton (Alice Springs); Leon Samsoneco (Alice Springs); Joe and Mary Groves (Woolner Station); Clive Hyde (NT News).

Ron Cross, Derick Plante, Bob Blackburn and Morio (Minolta Australia); Dick Bryant (Minolta, Japan); Renato Chua of Photokina (Minolta/Agfa, Philippines); Lisa Highton, Susan Tomnay, Clare Forte (Collins Publishers Australia).

Tim Cope wishes to acknowledge the following authors whose work has provided valuable assistance in the form of reference material:

Catherine Berndt, Ronald Berndt, Neville Cayley, John Coe, Douglas Lockwood, Eric Mack, Alan Moorehead, Alan Powell, Dick Roughsey and Vincent Serventy. Special thanks to Garry Dembon and Denise Kitchen and the contributors of Territory Editorial.